A Compendium of the Curious

A Miscellany of the Macabre, Mysterious, and Otherworldly

Max Gillespie-Martin

First published in the United Kingdom and Ireland by Kindle Direct Publishing 2023

ISBN 9798862205466

For my Friends & Family

Contents:

A Compendium of the Curious

Foreword

History, like an ancient tome with pages worn by time, holds within its folds tales of triumph and tragedy, heroes and villains, and the strange and macabre. It is a grand stage where humanity's darkest and most entertaining moments have played out over millennia. Welcome to a journey through history's shadowed alleyways, where the macabre and the entertaining converge to reveal the peculiar and often chilling facets of our shared past.

In these pages, we will venture beyond the well-trodden paths of history textbooks, beyond the names and dates that have long been etched into our collective memory. Instead, we will embark on a tour of the historical underbelly, where curiosity and a thirst for the bizarre guide our way. Prepare to be both horrified and captivated, for the stories we are about to uncover are not for the faint of heart.

The Allure of the Macabre

Why, you might ask, should we delve into the macabre side of history? It is a fair question, and the answer lies in our very nature. As humans, we are drawn to the mysterious, the eerie, and the unexplained. It is an intrinsic part of our psyche, an irresistible pull that has led generations to gather around campfires to share ghost stories and urban legends. Our fascination with the macabre stems from a deep-seated desire to confront our fears, to understand the unexplainable, and to find a sense of order in a chaotic world.

Moreover, the macabre is an essential thread in the tapestry of history itself. It reminds us that our past is not a sanitised, linear narrative of progress and enlightenment. It is, instead, a complex tapestry woven from the threads of human folly, superstition, and the unquenchable thirst for power. To explore the macabre is to acknowledge the darker aspects of our history, to confront the atrocities committed in the name of ideology, and to recognise that the human capacity for both greatness and depravity knows no bounds.

The Dark and the Entertaining

But this journey through history's macabre corridors is not intended to be a descent into despair. Quite the contrary, in fact. For alongside the unsettling tales of tragedy and horror, we will discover the peculiar and the absurd, the anecdotes that defy reason and yet never fail to amuse. It is the juxtaposition of the dark and the entertaining that makes this exploration so compelling.

Throughout history, Individuals and events have emerged that can only be described as both bizarre and captivating. From eccentric monarchs with peculiar obsessions to peculiar culinary creations that defy the palate, these stories reveal the remarkable diversity of the human psyche. As we delve into these narratives, you will find yourself alternately shuddering with unease and bursting into laughter, a testament to the multifaceted nature of our past.

Navigating the Twists and Turns

As we embark on this journey together, it is essential to remember that history is not a static landscape but a living, breathing entity. Our understanding of the past evolves with each discovery, each new piece of evidence unearthed from the sands of time. What may seem macabre or entertaining to us today may have held different meanings for those who lived through these events. Therefore, we must approach these tales with sensitivity and an awareness of the cultural and historical context in which they occurred.

It is also worth noting that history, like any good story, is subject to interpretation. The line between fact and legend can sometimes blur, and the truth may be hidden beneath layers of myth and folklore. As we navigate these twists and turns, I encourage you to embrace the uncertainty, to revel in the ambiguity, and to question the narratives that have been handed down through the generations.

The Chapters Ahead

In the chapters that follow, we will journey through time and space, exploring a wide array of historical oddities, curiosities, and enigmas. We will encounter eccentric monarchs, dabble in the mysterious world of alchemy, and witness the peculiarities of Victorian mourning customs. We will delve into the macabre world of medical history, where peculiar remedies and bizarre treatments once held sway. And we will explore the realm of the unexplained, from ancient curses to haunted castles.

But remember, dear reader, that the stories contained herein are not mere relics of the past. They are windows into the fundamental human experience, reminders that history is not a distant echo but a living testament to our shared journey. So, as we begin this expedition through the macabre and the entertaining, prepare yourself for a rollercoaster ride through the annals of history, where the strange, the chilling, and the bizarre await at every turn.

Buckle up, for the past is a dark and thrilling amusement park, and we are about to embark on the ride of a lifetime.

Enjoy yourself and do be careful...

Chapter One

The Long-Lost Lexicon - An A to Z of Forgotten Words

Alacrity denotes an action with a peculiar coupling of both anxious briskness and undeniable enthusiasm. For instance, one might accept an invitation to a party, hosted by an equally popular yet impatient individual, with a great deal of *alacrity.*

Badinage refers to a state of light-hearted and sincere conversation. One might engage in *badinage* when unexpectedly meeting an old friend.

Confabulation is simply the act of conversing but may more specifically refer to speaking with no real sense of purpose, nor even a foundation in honesty. A friend at the pub telling apocryphal stories may be engaging in *confabulation.*

Desuetude is the regretful sense of something having fallen into disrepair or a lack of practice. Perhaps intentionally, the word itself has arguable fallen into *desuetude.*

Encomium is a formal term used to denote an extraordinary amount of praise. It derives from the Ancient Greek word for 'festivity'. A well-respected individual who has recently passed away may be showered with *encomium.*

Facile is a damning term for something believed to be easy or trivial. A musician's flourishes on a piano may be brutally dismissed as *facile.*

Gourmand refers to the quality of gratuitous greed. Someone who engages in exorbitant gluttony is likely *gourmand.*

Heterodoxy is a combination of two Latin terms; 'hetero-' or 'different to', and '-doxy' or 'belonging to'. Accordingly, phrase is the direct opposite of 'orthodoxy'. A figure who directly and brazenly denies normality or common consensus may be described as *heterodox.*

Impecunious simply means short of money. Next time you're unable to afford something, remind yourself, you are not poor. You are *impecunious.*

Jussulent is a peculiar name for an object full of soup or broth. In the dark winter months, there are few things better to end the day than a *jussulent* bowl.

Krioboly is the ritual sacrifice of a large number of goats. How many goats? Up to you! Why sacrifice the goats? Also up to you! Whatever the reason, sometimes you might want to spend the day performing a *krioboly.*

Latibule is a formal name for a well-concealed hiding place. When playing a good old-fashioned game of Hide and Seek, it wise to find a secretive *latibule.*

Macellarious pertains to butchers, meat merchants, and their culinary practices. An animal rights activist might well have a bone to pick with a professional of the *macellarious* persuasion.

Noisome surprisingly has absolutely nothing to do with an acoustic sensation, and instead denotes a foul, offensive odour. A rotten egg can quote handily be described as *noisome.*

Obsequious is an apt term for an underling or servant who behaves in a grovelling and eager-to-please manner to an odious extent. Friends or followers who serve in a suspiciously enthusiastic fashion are *obsequious.*

Patration refers to the successful and valiant completion and/or perfection of a specific task. An Olympic gold medalist might aim for *patration* in their athletic pursuits.

Quaeritation is the habit of almost obsessively questioning and inquiring. Heterodox to the conventional wisdom of many adults, it is almost always a good idea to *quaeritate*. Heartfelt questioning and sincere inquiry of oneself and one's environment will only ever lead to a deeper, and more meaningful, relationship with the world and it's fascinating inhabitants.

Robleting is the act of deliberately leading someone astray. A cunning brigand might *roblet* an unsuspecting passer-by.

Stultifying something quite literally means 'making it stupid'. A chocolate teapot and paper armour are *stultified* objects.

Tantuple refers to the multiplication of a number by another given number. Long, arduous mathematical formulae may be presented in the form of tedious *tantuplication.*

Uglyography is a reasonably polite term for atrocious handwriting. Doctors - understandably - famous for their *uglyography.*

Vituperative people are those who always find a way to be needlessly cruel, critical, and harsh of others' achievements. A pointlessly scathing review of a child's artwork is nought but *vituperative.*

Welmish things are those that possess a pale, sickly hue. A withered slug, a deceased fish, and a congealed pool of vomit can all be considered as *welmish.*

Xenisation is the act of travelling around a region as a foreigner. Undertaking a pilgrimage through a different country while holding no currency or knowing no language is a form of *xenisation.*

Yabbering is the art of talking at length about nonsense. A skilled confabulator is likely a student of *yabbering.*

Zeptosecond is a minuscule measure of time; denoting roughly one sextillionth of a second. A *zeptosecond* is only marginally faster than a jiffy.

"The only true wisdom is in knowing you know nothing."
- Socrates

Chapter Two

Nature's Eccentricities

Raining Cats and Dogs - Strange Weather Phenomena

The Bizarre Phenomenon of "Blood Rain" in Kerala, 2001: A Mysterious Shower

In July 2001, the southern Indian state of Kerala was thrust into the spotlight due to a bewildering and unsettling natural phenomenon: "Blood Rain." For a span of several weeks, the skies over parts of Kerala rained not water but a mysterious reddish substance that appeared eerily similar to blood. This enigmatic event captured the imaginations of scientists, residents, and the media, sparking a wave of curiosity and concern.

The Beginning of the Blood Rain

The unusual meteorological event began on July 25, 2001, when residents of Kerala's Idukki district, particularly the towns of Changanassery and Vaikom, were taken aback by what seemed like rainwater tainted with blood. The phenomenon quickly spread to other areas, including Kottayam, which experienced one of the most significant episodes.

Locals who witnessed the "blood rain" were understandably alarmed and puzzled. The crimson-coloured droplets splattering the ground and staining clothing and vehicles bore an uncanny resemblance to blood, intensifying the intrigue surrounding the event.

Scientific Investigations and Speculations

As news of the blood rain spread, the Kerala State Pollution Control Board (KSPCB) and the Indian Meteorological Department (IMD) initiated investigations to unravel the mystery behind this macabre rainfall. One of the initial concerns was that the red substance might be a health hazard.

The KSPCB quickly ruled out industrial pollution as a possible cause, given that the affected areas did not house significant industries. Moreover, the rainwater's pH levels were found to be within the normal range, dispelling fears of acid rain. Scientists and meteorologists proposed various theories to explain the phenomenon, including the possibility of coloured pollutants in the atmosphere or unusual dust particles suspended in the air. The most prominent hypothesis centred around the presence of airborne spores from terrestrial algae or fungi.

A Natural Explanation Emerges

The turning point in solving the mystery came when scientists from the Tropical Botanic Garden and Research Institute (TBGRI) in Kerala collected samples of the red rainwater. Through microscopic examination, they discovered the presence of tiny, spherical particles resembling biological cells. The discovery of these particles raised eyebrows and led to speculation that the rain might be linked to extraterrestrial sources, such as meteorite dust or cometary material. Some even theorised that the red particles were alien microbes.
To explore the possibility of an extraterrestrial connection, the samples were subjected to advanced analytical techniques. The results, however, pointed to a terrestrial origin. The mysterious red particles were identified as fungal spores, suggesting that the rain's reddish hue was a result of biological matter.

A Peculiar Discovery

Further research conducted by Dr. Godfrey Louis and his team at the TBGRI revealed an even more astounding revelation. The fungal spores responsible for the red rain were unlike any known species on Earth. Dr. Louis named this enigmatic life form "*Rajasthania keratensis.*"
Rajasthania keratensis was unique in several aspects. Its ability to withstand extreme conditions, including high radiation levels,

made it a fascinating subject of study. The unusual morphology and resilience of these microorganisms added to the intrigue surrounding the blood rain phenomenon.

The Scientific Explanation

The prevailing scientific theory suggested that the fungal spores of *Rajasthania keratensis* were lifted from the Earth's surface by a powerful updraft and carried into the upper atmosphere. There, they encountered high-altitude winds that transported them across long distances.

When these spores eventually descended back to Earth, they did so along with rain. The exposure to the extreme conditions of the upper atmosphere could have caused the spores to mutate, leading to their distinct red coloration. As they fell to the ground with raindrops, they gave rise to the phenomenon of "blood rain."

The Blood Rain Legacy

The episode of "blood rain" in Kerala left an indelible mark on both scientific research and popular culture. It challenged our understanding of atmospheric processes and demonstrated the resilience of life forms even in extreme conditions.

The discovery of *Rajasthania keratensis* prompted further research into extremophiles—organisms capable of thriving in harsh environments. Additionally, it ignited debates about the possibility of life existing in outer space, given the spores' ability to survive in the upper atmosphere.

Ball Lightning: Unraveling the Enigmatic Luminous Spheres

The world of atmospheric phenomena is filled with mysteries, but perhaps none are as captivating and elusive as ball lightning. These luminous orbs, resembling floating spheres of light, have puzzled scientists and eyewitnesses for centuries. With their unpredictable behaviour and transient existence, ball lightning remains one of the most enigmatic natural phenomena.

A History of Enigma

The first documented accounts of ball lightning date back centuries, with some of the earliest reports originating in Europe and Asia. Notably, the natural philosopher Georg Wilhelm Richmann met a tragic end in 1753 while attempting to study ball lightning. Struck and killed during an experiment in St. Petersburg, Russia, Richmann's untimely demise underscored the mysterious and potentially dangerous nature of this phenomenon.

Throughout history, eyewitnesses have described ball lightning in various ways. Common characteristics include its spherical shape, luminosity, and erratic movement. Witnesses often recount tales of ball lightning entering buildings, aircraft, or vehicles, leaving a trail of damage or burning before vanishing, either quietly or explosively.

Scientific Quest for Understanding

Despite the numerous eyewitness accounts, ball lightning remains a scientific puzzle. Its fleeting and unpredictable nature has posed significant challenges to researchers. As a result, it has been a subject of much debate and speculation within the scientific community.

Theories and Hypotheses

Scientists have proposed various theories to explain the origin and nature of ball lightning, but none have been universally accepted. Some of the prominent hypotheses include:

- Plasma Spheroids: This theory suggests that ball lightning consists of hot, ionised gas or plasma. It attempts to explain the luminosity and longevity of ball lightning but faces challenges in accounting for its unique behaviour.
- Microwave Radiation: Researchers have proposed that ball lightning may be formed by microwave radiation during thunderstorms. However, this theory lacks concrete evidence and has not gained widespread acceptance.
- Chemical Reactions: Another theory posits that chemical reactions within thunderstorms may create ball lightning. While this idea offers a plausible explanation for the phenomenon's appearance, it remains speculative and requires further investigation.

Laboratory Reproduction

Despite the difficulties in studying natural ball lightning, some researchers have managed to reproduce ball lightning-like phenomena in laboratory settings. These artificially created "plasma balls" share certain characteristics with naturally occurring ball lightning, providing valuable insights into the possible mechanisms behind this phenomenon.

It's essential to note that encounters with ball lightning are rare, and they typically do not pose significant threats to human safety. While some eyewitness accounts describe ball lightning causing minor damage, such as scorch marks, it is generally not considered a major hazard. In most cases, ball lightning appears and disappears without causing harm.

Seeking Answers

The study of ball lightning continues to be a challenging and evolving field. Scientists are intrigued by this phenomenon not only for its scientific significance but also because of its potential implications for understanding other atmospheric and celestial phenomena. As our knowledge of plasma physics, atmospheric chemistry, and electromagnetic interactions deepens, we inch closer to unravelling the mysteries of ball lightning.

One of the key areas of research related to ball lightning is the study of plasmas. Plasma, often referred to as the fourth state of matter, is a collection of charged particles, including ions and electrons. Ball lightning is thought to be composed of plasma, and understanding the behaviour of plasmas under various conditions is essential to comprehending this phenomenon.

The chemical reactions that occur within thunderstorms and their potential role in the formation of ball lightning remain subjects of investigation. Researchers are exploring the possibility that specific chemical reactions in the atmosphere could create the conditions necessary for the emergence of ball lightning.

Another avenue of research focuses on the electromagnetic interactions that may be at play during the formation and behaviour of ball lightning. This includes studying how lightning and thunderstorms generate electromagnetic fields and how these fields could influence the appearance and movement of ball lightning.

Bizarre Rainbow Anomalies: Nature's Colourful Oddities

Rainbows, those stunning arcs of prismatic light that grace our skies after rainfall, are well-known natural wonders. However, there are times when nature decides to throw a curveball, creating bizarre and hypnotic rainbow anomalies that leave observers puzzled and awestruck.

1. Supernumerary Rainbows

Rainbows are typically characterised by seven distinct colours, but occasionally, nature offers an extra treat: supernumerary rainbows. These additional, closely spaced rainbows are fainter and occur inside the primary rainbow. They are the result of light wave interference and diffraction.
Supernumerary rainbows display bands of pastel colours, appearing as faint, ghostly echoes of the main rainbow. Observing them is a rare and ethereal experience, as they challenge our perception of the classic rainbow's uniformity.

2. Moonbows: Moonlit Magic

Rainbows are typically daytime phenomena, relying on sunlight to refract and create their vibrant colours. However, moonbows, also known as lunar rainbows or white rainbows, are a captivating exception. Moonbows occur when moonlight refracts through raindrops, creating a pale, silvery arc against a dark night sky.
Moonbows are elusive and are often seen in tranquil, misty settings, like waterfalls or coastal areas. Their soft, otherworldly beauty has inspired awe and wonder throughout history, as they illuminate the night with a touch of celestial magic.

3. Circumhorizontal Arcs: Fire Rainbows

One of the most striking and vivid rainbow anomalies is the circumhorizontal arc, colloquially known as the fire rainbow. Unlike traditional rainbows, which are circular arcs, fire rainbows appear as horizontal, blazing bands of colour in the sky.

These vibrant arcs form when sunlight passes through hexagonal ice crystals in cirrus clouds. The crystal alignment and refraction angle create this fiery spectacle, which can be even more brilliant than regular rainbows.

4. Fogbows: Ghostly White Rainbows

Fogbows, also called white rainbows or cloudbows, are the ethereal cousins of rainbows. They appear as pale, almost colourless bows against a background of thick fog or mist. Unlike rainbows, which form through refraction and dispersion, fogbows are the result of diffraction.

The tiny water droplets in fog are responsible for creating fogbows. These droplets are so small that they diffract sunlight, rather than refract it, resulting in the pale, ghostly appearance of fogbows.

5. Red Rainbows: Rare and Radiant

While the familiar hues of a rainbow include red, there are rare instances when the entire rainbow spectrum is filtered out, leaving only a stunning red rainbow. This phenomenon occurs when the sky is dominated by colours at the blue end of the spectrum, and only red light remains to form the rainbow.

Red rainbows are indeed rare and have been documented as awe-inspiring anomalies. Their striking crimson hues are a testament to the fascinating interplay of light and atmospheric conditions.

6. Twinned Rainbows: Nature's Mirrors

Double rainbows are relatively common and occur when light is reflected twice inside raindrops. But even rarer are twinned rainbows, which appear as two rainbows of similar intensity and colour, separated by a distinct dark band of sky.

Twinned rainbows are created by the complex interplay of reflection and refraction within raindrops. They are captivating anomalies that add an extra layer of intrigue to the already mesmerising world of rainbows.

7. Upside-Down Rainbows: The Circumzenithal Arc

Imagine looking up to the sky and seeing a radiant, upside-down rainbow curving above you. This phenomenon is known as the circumzenithal arc, and it is a celestial spectacle that occurs when sunlight is refracted through horizontally oriented ice crystals.

The circumzenithal arc's vibrant colours and celestial position make it a breathtaking and somewhat surreal anomaly. Observers often find themselves gazing upward, captivated by this upside-down rainbow.

The Hessdalen Lights - Norway's Enigmatic Luminescent Mystery

In the remote valley of Hessdalen, Norway, a perplexing and captivating phenomenon has captured the imagination of scientists and enthusiasts alike–the Hessdalen Lights. These mysterious and elusive luminous orbs have been a subject of intrigue and investigation since they were first reported in the early 1980s.

A Phenomenon in the Norwegian Night Sky

Nestled within the picturesque Hessdalen Valley, a rural area in central Norway, the Hessdalen Lights have defied easy explanation for decades. Eyewitnesses describe them as luminous, floating orbs that range from the size of a football to several meters in diameter. These orbs radiate a soft, pulsating glow and often appear as shimmering, multicoloured lights in the night sky.

The first documented reports of the Hessdalen Lights date back to the early 1980s when local residents and tourists began noticing these unusual luminous phenomena. Over time, the sightings became more frequent, captivating the attention of the scientific community.

Scientific Investigations

The Hessdalen Lights quickly became a subject of scientific inquiry, with researchers and experts from around the world drawn to the valley to study the phenomenon. Several key aspects of these investigations include:

One of the most intriguing aspects of the Hessdalen Lights is their persistence and regularity. Unlike many other unexplained phenomena, these lights appear frequently, sometimes nightly, making them a prime candidate for systematic observation and study.

Researchers in Hessdalen have employed state-of-the-art technology, including cameras, spectrographs, and magnetometers, to capture data and analyse the lights. These tools have provided valuable insights into the characteristics of the phenomenon.

Hypotheses and Theories

Numerous hypotheses have been proposed to explain the Hessdalen Lights, but none have provided a definitive answer. Some of the prominent theories include:

Plasma Phenomenon

One prevailing theory suggests that the Hessdalen Lights are a type of plasma phenomenon. Plasma, the fourth state of matter, is composed of charged particles and can emit light when excited. Researchers have explored the possibility that natural plasma formations in the valley are responsible for the luminous orbs.

Geological Activity

The presence of various minerals in the valley has led to speculation that geological activity, such as piezoelectricity or triboluminescence, might play a role in generating the lights. These processes involve the release of energy through mechanical stress or friction and could potentially explain some of the observed phenomena.

Combination of Factors

It is possible that the Hessdalen Lights result from a combination of factors, including atmospheric conditions, geological processes, and the unique topography of the valley. Some researchers believe that a holistic approach, considering multiple factors simultaneously, may hold the key to understanding this complex phenomenon.

Unusual Tornadoes: Firenadoes and Beyond

Tornadoes are one of the most formidable and awe-inspiring natural phenomena on Earth. These violent, twisting columns of air can cause immense destruction and chaos. While traditional tornadoes are frightening enough, some tornado variants defy expectations and add an extra layer of peculiarity to nature's tempestuous displays.

The Basics of Tornadoes

Before delving into unusual tornadoes, it's essential to understand the basics of these powerful whirlwinds. Tornadoes typically form from severe thunderstorms when certain atmospheric conditions are present. Warm, moist air colliding with cool, dry air can create the instability necessary for tornado formation.

Firenadoes: The Fiery Tempests

A firenado, short for "fire tornado" or "fire whirl," is a rare and horrifying phenomenon that occurs when a tornado and a wildfire collide. These ferocious fire whirls are an unnerving blend of the destructive forces of fire and wind.

Firenadoes are typically spawned from intense wildfires or wildfires exhibiting pyrocumulonimbus clouds. These storms can generate powerful updrafts and create firenado conditions. When strong, rotating updrafts meet the flames of a wildfire, a firenado can form. These whirlwinds can reach immense heights, with swirling flames creating a terrifying spectacle.

The destructive capability of firenadoes is immense. They can hurl burning debris great distances, making firefighting efforts even more challenging and dangerous. The intense heat and shifting winds within a firenado can exacerbate wildfire conditions, spreading the blaze further.

Haboobs: Dust Storm Tornadoes

Haboobs, also known as dust storms or sandstorms, are colossal walls of dust and sand that sweep across arid regions. These massive dust storms can sometimes produce tornado-like features, earning them the nickname "dust storm tornadoes."

Haboobs can generate powerful wind gusts that create dust whirlwinds resembling tornadoes. While they may not possess the same destructive force as traditional tornadoes, these dust storm tornadoes can still pose hazards to visibility and property.

Waterspouts: Tornadoes Over Water

Waterspouts are tornadoes that form over bodies of water. They share many characteristics with their land-based counterparts but have unique attributes due to their aquatic environment.

Waterspouts can form in two primary ways: as tornadic waterspouts or fair-weather waterspouts. Tornadic waterspouts are associated with severe thunderstorms and possess the same destructive potential as land tornadoes. In contrast, fair-weather waterspouts develop in calmer conditions and are typically less powerful.

While waterspouts are relatively common in some parts of the world, witnessing one is still considered a rare and unusual occurrence. These aquatic tornadoes often leave witnesses in awe of nature's power.

Snow Tornadoes: Icy Whirlwinds

In cold regions, particularly during the winter months, a peculiar meteorological phenomenon known as snow devils or snow whirlwinds can occur. These frosty cousins of tornadoes form when cold air masses meet warmer ground temperatures. Snow tornadoes are generally less intense than their warmer-weather counterparts and are unlikely to cause significant damage. However, they are visually striking and a reminder that tornado-like phenomena can occur in a variety of climates.

Nature's Myriad of Twists and Turns

Tornadoes are among nature's most impressive and terrifying displays of power, and their unusual variants only add to their mystique. From firenadoes that merge fire and wind to dust storm tornadoes in arid landscapes and the icy twists of snow tornadoes, these meteorological marvels remind us of the complex and unpredictable nature of our planet's weather systems.

As we delve into the world of unusual tornadoes, we are reminded that nature's forces are boundless and capable of producing phenomena that both astound and humble us. The study and understanding of these tornado variants continue to be a vital field of meteorological research, shedding light on the ever-evolving mysteries of our dynamic planet.

Whether we gaze upon a firenado's menacing flames or witness a snow tornado's gentle whirlwind dance, these unusual tornadoes serve as a reminder that, in the world of weather, the unexpected is always just around the corner.

The Hum: Unraveling the Sonic Anomaly

In scattered locations around the world, a peculiar and persistent sonic phenomenon known as "the Hum" has confounded residents and researchers alike. Described as a low-frequency, incessant, and often maddening sound, the Hum has garnered attention for decades.

The Perplexing Sound of the Hum

Imagine living in a world where you are constantly accompanied by a low, monotonous sound that never seems to fade away. This is the daily reality for those who experience the Hum, a sound that is often likened to the idling of a distant engine or a deep vibration.
Reports of the Hum have surfaced in various countries, from the United States and the United Kingdom to New Zealand and Canada. The Hum knows no boundaries, affecting people in urban and rural areas alike.

The History of the Hum

While the Hum's origins are shrouded in mystery, reports of the phenomenon began emerging in the mid-20th century. Early instances of the Hum were often dismissed as auditory hallucinations or the result of industrial activity.
Over the years, the Hum persisted, with individuals and communities reporting the phenomenon and its associated discomfort. Investigations into the source of the Hum yielded inconclusive results, further deepening the mystery.

Scientific Investigations

Scientists and researchers have made efforts to analyse the Hum, recording its characteristics and attempting to pinpoint its source. The Hum is typically described as a low-frequency sound, often between 30 and 80 Hz, which places it in the infrasound range, below the threshold of human hearing.

The quest to identify the source of the Hum has led to various hypotheses. Some researchers have suggested that industrial equipment, such as ventilation systems or compressors, might be responsible. Others have explored natural phenomena like geological activity or atmospheric pressure changes as potential causes.

Living with the persistent Hum can have psychological and physiological effects on those affected. Insomnia, anxiety, and stress have been reported, and the constant presence of the sound can be deeply unsettling.

In some regions, communities have rallied together to address the issue of the Hum. Residents have shared their experiences, organised meetings, and petitioned local authorities to investigate the phenomenon.

The Elusive Source

Despite decades of investigation, the source of the Hum remains elusive. Researchers continue to grapple with the challenge of identifying and mitigating the phenomenon.

Efforts to mitigate the impact of the Hum have included soundproofing homes, using white noise machines, or seeking refuge in noise-canceling headphones. However, these solutions offer temporary relief rather than a permanent remedy.

The Enigmatic Dancing Forests of Russia

In a remote corner of Russia's Kaliningrad Oblast, a truly bizarre and captivating natural wonder exists—the Dancing Forest. This unique woodland, located on the Curonian Spit, has puzzled scientists and enchanted visitors for generations.

The Enchanted Curonian Spit

The Curonian Spit is a narrow, sandy peninsula stretching along the Baltic Sea. Known for its diverse ecosystems and stunning landscapes, it is home to a natural anomaly that defies explanation—the Dancing Forest.

What sets the Dancing Forest apart are its peculiar pine trees, their trunks and branches warped and twisted into seemingly unnatural shapes. Some appear to bend like arched bridges, while others contort in spirals and loops. The forest creates an otherworldly and eerie atmosphere.

Natural or Supernatural?

The bizarre shapes of the trees have fuelled numerous legends and myths about the forest. Locals have attributed the phenomenon to everything from supernatural forces to alien visitors. However, scientific investigations offer a more rational explanation.

One of the leading theories proposes that strong prevailing winds from the nearby Baltic Sea are responsible for the contorted shapes of the trees. These relentless winds may twist and shape the growing trees over time, gradually molding them into their peculiar forms.

Another theory suggests that the composition of the soil in the Dancing Forest may play a role. The sandy, unstable ground could lead to uneven root growth, causing the trees to bend and twist in their pursuit of stability and nutrients.

A Unique Destination

The Dancing Forest has become a tourist attraction, drawing visitors from around the world who are eager to witness the strange spectacle for themselves. Guided tours are available to explore the forest, providing insights into its history and ecological significance.

Efforts to protect the Dancing Forest and the fragile ecosystem of the Curonian Spit have been ongoing. Conservationists work diligently to preserve this natural wonder while allowing visitors to experience its magic.

The Ongoing Mystery

While scientific theories offer plausible explanations for the Dancing Forest's unique trees, the full story remains an ongoing mystery. Researchers continue to study the forest, collecting data and monitoring tree growth to better understand the processes at play.

The Dancing Forest serves as a captivating example of nature's complexity and capacity to produce extraordinary and unexpected phenomena. It reminds us that our planet is full of wonders, both known and yet to be discovered.

The Emu War - Feathered Foes and Fowl Play

Across military history, there are tales of epic battles, heroic feats, and moments of sheer absurdity. Among these, the Emu War of 1932 stands out as a prime example of when the animal kingdom took on the might of the military, and well, feathers flew!

The Emu Invasion

Our story begins in the vast, arid plains of Western Australia, where the picturesque backdrop of farms and wheat fields played host to an unexpected menace: emus. Yes, those flightless, long-legged birds with a penchant for pecking their way through crops had declared war on the farmers.
The problem? Emus were on the march, descending upon the wheat fields in droves, ravaging the crops, and leaving a trail of agricultural devastation in their wake. The farmers were desperate, and something had to be done to stem the feathered tide.

Enter the Military

In a plot twist that could only happen in the world of bizarre history, the Australian government decided that the solution to the emu problem lay not in traditional pest control methods but in the military might of the Commonwealth.
And so, Major G.P.W. Meredith of the Royal Australian Artillery, along with two soldiers armed with two Lewis machine guns and 10,000 rounds of ammunition, was dispatched to deal with the marauding emus. It was a true David-and-Goliath scenario, except this time, Goliath had machine guns, and David was a 5-foot-tall flightless bird.

The Battle Commences

November 2, 1932, marked the beginning of the Emu War, as the military rolled out its secret weapon – the machine guns. With confidence befitting a military campaign, the soldiers set

out to mow down the emu hordes and save the wheat fields from certain doom.
But the emus, as it turns out, were formidable opponents. They were fast, agile, and surprisingly resilient. As the soldiers opened fire, the emus scattered in all directions, evading the hail of bullets. It was like trying to hit a moving target at a carnival shooting range, but with real consequences for the crops.

Tactical Retreat
After the initial skirmish, the emus retreated into the wilderness, regrouping for what would become a series of hit-and-run guerrilla tactics. The soldiers, on the other hand, were left scratching their heads and wondering how they had underestimated their feathered adversaries.
The emus proved adept at dodging bullets and mocking the military's attempts to control them. They even showed a remarkable ability to take hits and keep on running, leading one to wonder if they were, in fact, the descendants of some prehistoric, bulletproof bird.

The Great Emu Chase
As the battle unfolded, Major Meredith and his men found themselves engaged in a bizarre game of cat and mouse with the emus. They would drive their trucks to catch up with the emus, set up the machine guns, and fire away, only for the emus to scatter in every direction, leaving a trail of dust and disappointment.
The soldiers' enthusiasm began to wane as their ammunition dwindled, and they realised that they were burning through precious rounds without making a significant dent in the emu population. To add insult to injury, the emus seemed to mock them with their comical, head-bobbing gait.
By December 10, 1932, after a month of battling emus and suffering numerous defeats, Major Meredith decided that

perhaps discretion was the better part of valour. He ordered a strategic retreat, admitting that the emus had won the battle.
In a telegram to the authorities, he humorously declared, "The emu command had evidently ordered guerrilla tactics, and its unwieldy army soon split up into innumerable small units that made use of their military equipment by manoeuvring detached for the most part and thus distracted our pursuit over a large area."

The Aftermath

The Emu War came to an ignominious end, with the emus victorious and the military's reputation slightly tarnished. The Australian government officially withdrew its troops from the frontlines, leaving the emus to continue their wheat field raiding at will.
In the end, it was not the might of the military that prevailed but the cunning and resilience of the emus. The farmers, however, were left to contend with the aftermath of the emu invasion, and the war remains a quirky footnote in Australian history.
The Emu War, while a humorous and bizarre episode, does carry some valuable lessons. It serves as a reminder that nature can sometimes defy human attempts at control and that even the most well-equipped armies can be outwitted by determined foes.

"Emus are little more than feathered stomachs borne on mighty legs and ruled by a tiny brain."
- Richard Fortey

Poisonous Plants - Mother Nature's Dark Sense of Humour

Plants, with their vibrant colours and delicate petals, can be nature's way of telling us that beauty can be deceiving. In this chapter, we'll explore a miscellany of toxic and poisonous plants from around the world. These botanical baddies remind us that even in the plant kingdom, Mother Nature has a rather dark and ironic sense of humour.

Deadly Nightshade - The Femme Fatale of the Plant World

Deadly Nightshade is an herbaceous perennial that stands about three to five feet tall. Its leaves are large, heart-shaped, and deep green, while its distinctive bell-shaped flowers come in shades of purple, giving the plant an alluring and deceptively beautiful appearance.

The name "belladonna" is derived from Italian, meaning "beautiful woman." In ancient times, the plant was used cosmetically, as the juice from its berries was employed to dilate the pupils, creating the appearance of larger, more seductive eyes. However, this practice was extremely dangerous and often led to poisoning.

Potent Presence

The true danger of Deadly Nightshade lies in its alkaloid content, particularly scopolamine, hyoscyamine, and atropine. These chemicals are potent and can cause a range of adverse effects when ingested or absorbed through the skin.

Ingesting even a small amount of Deadly Nightshade can lead to a host of severe symptoms, including blurred vision, hallucinations, delirium, seizures, paralysis, and, in extreme cases, death. The plant's toxicity is such that its ingestion should be considered a medical emergency.

Throughout history, Deadly Nightshade has earned a notorious reputation as a poison of choice for assassins and those seeking to harm others. The plant's deadly properties have been used in a variety of dark and sinister ways, from poison-tipped arrows to concoctions meant to eliminate political rivals. Paradoxically, Deadly Nightshade has also found its place in the history of medicine. In carefully controlled doses, some of its alkaloids, such as atropine, have been used to treat various medical conditions, including gastrointestinal disorders and certain types of poisoning. However, these applications are highly specialised and should only be administered by medical professionals.

The Devious Beauty of the Castor Bean Plant

The castor bean plant is a large, fast-growing shrub that can reach heights of up to twelve feet. Its distinctive leaves are palmate, with several pointed lobes radiating from a central stem. The plant produces clusters of spiky, green seed capsules, each containing multiple seeds. These seeds are where the danger lies.

The castor bean plant has a rich history of human use, dating back thousands of years. Historically, castor oil, derived from the plant's seeds, was used for medicinal purposes, including as a laxative. However, the seeds themselves contain a deadly toxin, ricin, which has earned the plant its sinister reputation.

Toxic Subterfuge

Ricin is a highly toxic protein that can disrupt cellular function and lead to severe illness or death. A small amount of ricin, when ingested, inhaled, or injected, can have deadly consequences. Ricin poisoning can manifest with a range of symptoms, including nausea, vomiting, abdominal pain, diarrhoea, seizures, and organ failure. Without prompt medical intervention, ricin poisoning can be fatal.

The deadly potential of ricin has not gone unnoticed by those seeking to harm others. Throughout history, the toxin has been used in various assassination attempts and acts of espionage. Its potency and difficulty to detect have made it an attractive weapon for those with malicious intent.

In modern times, awareness of the dangers posed by ricin is critical. Security measures are in place to monitor and control the handling of castor bean plants and their seeds to prevent misuse. Education and training are essential to ensure that individuals working with these plants understand the associated risks.

The Unexpected Upside

Despite its lethal potential, castor oil derived from castor bean seeds has controlled medicinal and industrial applications. It is used in various products, including pharmaceuticals, cosmetics, and lubricants. However, these applications involve highly refined and purified forms of the oil, with ricin removed.

The Deceptive Allure of Water Hemlock

Water hemlock is a perennial plant that typically grows in moist habitats, near streams, ponds, and wetlands. Its tall stems are adorned with umbrella-like clusters of tiny white flowers, creating an elegant and deceptively attractive appearance.
The plant's name, "water hemlock," is derived from its habitat and its resemblance to true hemlock trees. It has a significant place in history, primarily as a dangerous and deadly plant.

A Nervous Disposition

Water hemlock is infamous for containing cicutoxin, a highly toxic alkaloid that affects the central nervous system. Ingesting any part of the plant, especially the roots, can result in rapid and severe poisoning. Water hemlock poisoning leads to a range of symptoms, including nausea, vomiting, abdominal pain, tremors, seizures, and death in severe cases. The rapid onset and severity of symptoms make it one of the most dangerous plant poisonings in North America.
Throughout history, water hemlock has been used as a potent poison. It is believed to have been used in assassination attempts and as a means of eliminating enemies. The plant's high toxicity and the availability of its roots have made it an attractive choice for those seeking a lethal weapon.
Indigenous peoples in North America have recognised the dangers of water hemlock for centuries. Some tribes used it for hunting by contaminating bait with water hemlock, thereby poisoning the animals they sought to catch.

Under New Management

In modern times, awareness of the dangers posed by water hemlock is crucial. Educating individuals about the plant's characteristics and the severe consequences of ingestion is a key aspect of prevention.
Efforts are made to control and eradicate water hemlock in areas where it poses a threat to livestock and human safety.

Identifying and removing the plants from potential contact with humans and animals is a priority.

Manchineel Tree: The Forbidden Apple of Death

In the idyllic landscapes of the Caribbean, a perilous presence is concealed among the lush greenery—the manchineel tree (*Hippomane mancinella*). Despite its tropical beauty, this tree is renowned as one of the most poisonous in the world.

The manchineel tree is a small to medium-sized evergreen tree native to the Caribbean, as well as parts of Central and South America. Its dark green leaves and small, greenish-yellow fruit give it an unassuming and picturesque appearance.

Bad Reputation

Throughout history, the manchineel tree has been known by various names, including "beach apple" and "death apple." These monikers reflect the perilous reputation it has earned due to its highly toxic nature.

The manchineel tree produces a milky white sap that contains a potent mix of toxins, including phorbol and various organic compounds. All parts of the tree, including its fruit, leaves, and bark, are laced with this lethal sap. Contact with any part of the manchineel tree can result in severe skin reactions, including blistering and burning. Ingesting even a small amount of its fruit can lead to agonising symptoms, such as abdominal pain, vomiting, diarrhoea, and potentially fatal complications.

Indigenous peoples in the Caribbean have long been aware of the dangers posed by the manchineel tree. They have used its toxic sap to poison arrows and darts for hunting and warfare.

Local communities have taken steps to raise awareness about the manchineel tree's dangers. Signs and warnings often accompany its presence on beaches and in coastal areas, alerting visitors to its toxic nature.

Oleander: The Beautiful Poison

In gardens around the world, the oleander (*Nerium oleander*) stands as a striking testament to nature's capacity for beauty and peril. With its vibrant, showy flowers and evergreen foliage, this shrub is a popular choice for ornamental planting. However, beneath its charming exterior, the oleander conceals a deadly secret.

Oleander is a hardy, evergreen shrub that boasts an abundance of colourful, trumpet-shaped flowers. These blossoms come in various shades, including white, pink, and red, creating a captivating and picturesque display. Its lush foliage and fragrant blooms make it a popular choice for gardens, parks, and landscapes.

Lethal Appeal

Throughout history, oleander has been valued for its aesthetic appeal. It has been used in various cultures for decorative purposes, adorning gardens and outdoor spaces with its vibrant blooms. Beneath its vibrant exterior, oleander harbours a potent mix of toxic compounds, including oleandrin and nerioside. These chemicals affect the heart and other vital organs, and they can lead to severe poisoning.

Ingesting any part of the oleander plant can result in a range of symptoms, including nausea, vomiting, diarrhoea, irregular heart rhythms, and, in severe cases, death. Oleander poisoning is considered a medical emergency and requires immediate treatment.

The Usual Suspect

Oleander has a place in various cultures' folklore, often as a symbol of danger or ill omens. In some regions, it has been associated with superstitions and beliefs about its toxic properties.

Historical accounts attest to the dangers of oleander. Instances of accidental poisoning and misguided use in traditional medicine have been documented.

In modern times, educational campaigns aim to inform the public about the dangers of oleander. These initiatives stress the importance of avoiding contact with the plant and its products. Gardeners and landscapers are encouraged to exercise caution when planting oleander, especially in areas frequented by children and pets. Proper labelling and awareness can prevent accidental ingestions.

The Enigmatic Effects of Angel's Trumpet

The angel's trumpet (*Brugmansia spp.*) has long captivated those who encounter its exquisite blossoms and intoxicating fragrance. However, beneath its enchanting allure lies a dark secret—the plant's toxicity.

Angel's trumpet is renowned for its stunning, trumpet-shaped flowers that hang pendulously in a variety of hues, emitting a bewitching fragrance. Its aesthetic beauty and fragrant blooms have earned it a place in gardens and landscapes worldwide. Throughout history, angel's trumpet has adorned outdoor spaces, enchanting onlookers with its lush foliage and striking blossoms. Its presence has inspired stories, folklore, and artistic interpretations.

Beneath its captivating exterior, angel's trumpet contains toxic alkaloids, including scopolamine, atropine, and hyoscyamine. These chemicals can have profound effects on the central nervous system when ingested or absorbed through the skin.

The effects of angel's trumpet toxicity can range from mild to severe, and they may include:

- Hallucinations: Individuals exposed to the plant may experience vivid and often disturbing hallucinations. These hallucinations can blur the line between reality and fantasy.
- Confusion: Cognitive impairment and confusion are common symptoms, making it difficult for affected individuals to distinguish between what is real and what is imagined.
- Paralysis: Muscle weakness and paralysis may occur, affecting mobility and coordination.
- Seizures: In severe cases, seizures can manifest, posing a significant risk to the affected individual's well-being.
- Coma and Death: Ingesting large amounts of angel's trumpet or experiencing severe poisoning can lead to a coma and, in extreme cases, death.

Throughout history, the angel's trumpet has been linked to stories of enchantment and allure, often symbolising danger and temptation. Its intoxicating fragrance and striking appearance have inspired tales of bewitching encounters. Historical records bear witness to the dangers associated with angel's trumpet. Accidental ingestions, misguided use in traditional medicine, and cases of poisoning have been documented.

Doll's Eye Plant: The Eye-Catching, Brain-Tickling Herb

In the world of peculiar plants, the Doll's Eye (*Actaea pachypoda*) stands out as a real head-turner, quite literally. With its distinctive white berries that bear a striking resemblance to tiny eyeballs, this plant is both enchanting and bewitching. However, beneath its whimsical exterior, it conceals some rather quirky effects.

Doll's Eye is a woodland perennial plant native to North America. Its most eye-catching feature, quite literally, is its white berries adorned with a prominent black dot, resembling miniature doll's eyes. These berries make the plant an unusual and attention-grabbing addition to the natural world.

Throughout history, Doll's Eye has attracted attention for its distinctive appearance. It has been the subject of folklore, curiosity, and no small amount of wonder.

A Secret Admirer

The name "Doll's Eye" hints at the quirky effects associated with this plant. In particular, the berries contain compounds called cardiogenic toxins, which can have some rather interesting effects on the body.

Consuming Doll's Eye berries can lead to symptoms that include dizziness, nausea, and even the sensation of walking on uneven ground. Imagine taking a stroll, feeling like you're on a whimsical, wobbly adventure through a fairytale forest.

In addition to the wobbles, some individuals report experiencing blurred vision or a "double vision" effect after consuming Doll's Eye berries. It's as though they've entered a surreal world with multiple perspectives.

The most bizarre effect of Doll's Eye is the dilation of the pupils, which can make a person's eyes appear as though they are those of a doll. It's like an impromptu, nature-inspired costume change.

Doll's Eye has earned a place in folklore and curious anecdotes, often associated with its unique appearance and peculiar effects. It has inspired tales of enchantment and wonder, adding a touch of whimsy to the natural world. Throughout history, Doll's Eye has been both admired and respected for its eccentricity. Its berries have been the subject of many conversations and even provided inspiration for creative minds.

Rat Kings - The Twisted Tails of Rodent Royalty

In the realm of the macabre and the bizarre, few phenomena are as simultaneously unsettling and captivating as the Rat King. These peculiar formations, consisting of multiple rats tangled together by their tails, have captured the imaginations of naturalists, folklore enthusiasts, and curious minds for centuries.

The Enigmatic Rat King

A Rat King is not an actual rat of royalty but rather a term used to describe a cluster of rats whose tails have become entangled, creating a bizarre and grotesque union. The resulting formation can range from a few rats to a larger assembly, all bound together in an intricate knot of fur, tails, and sometimes even blood.

Historical Accounts

The earliest known accounts of Rat Kings date back to the 16th century in Europe. These mysterious entanglements were often interpreted as dark omens, and their discovery was met with a mixture of fascination and fear.

One of the most famous historical instances occurred in 1828 in Germany when a Rat King comprising 32 rats was found in a miller's barn. The discovery ignited public interest, and the specimen was preserved for scientific study.

Scientific Explanations

The scientific explanation for Rat Kings revolves around a combination of natural factors, rather than supernatural forces. While the exact cause is still debated, several theories have been proposed:

Sticky Substances: It's believed that the rats' tails become entangled when they come into contact with a sticky or adhesive substance, such as sap or gum. As the rats groom themselves and their fellow rats, their tails can become matted together over time.

Crowded Living Conditions: In densely populated rat colonies, close quarters and competition for resources can lead to rats coming into contact with each other's tails more frequently, increasing the likelihood of entanglement.

Disease and Parasites: Some researchers suggest that disease or parasites could weaken the rats, making them less capable of untangling their tails when they become stuck together.

While Rat Kings have long been associated with superstition and folklore, modern science has shed light on the phenomenon. It's important to note that Rat Kings are extremely rare and occur under unusual circumstances. Most rats do not experience this bizarre fate.

The Folklore and Superstition

Rat Kings have long been the subject of superstition and folklore, often associated with dark omens and ill fortune. In some cultures, the discovery of a Rat King was believed to foretell famine, pestilence, or political upheaval. In contrast, other traditions saw Rat Kings as having magical or supernatural significance.

Despite their eerie reputation, Rat Kings have garnered fascination from collectors and museums over the years. Preserved specimens, like the one from Germany in 1828, have found their way into natural history collections, where they serve as both scientific curiosities and cultural artefacts.

The enigmatic Rat King has made appearances in literature, art, and popular culture, where it continues to capture the imagination of creators and audiences alike. Whether as a symbol of the bizarre or a source of horror, Rat Kings persist as a unique and enduring theme.

Literature: Rat Kings have made appearances in literature, including works of fiction and horror. They often serve as eerie and unsettling elements in stories that explore the boundaries of the strange and supernatural.

Art: Artists have depicted Rat Kings in various forms, from paintings to sculptures, exploring their eerie and symbolic aspects.

"Nobody near me here, but rats, and they are fine stealthy secret fellows."
- *Charles Dickens*

Puppeteers of the Animal Kingdom - Mind-Controlling Parasites

Nature is a theatre of extraordinary adaptations, where countless organisms have evolved intricate strategies for survival. Among these adaptations, some of the most eerie and captivating are the parasites that manipulate the minds of their hosts.

Mind-controlling parasites are a diverse group of organisms, including bacteria, fungi, protozoa, and insects, each with its own unique methods of control. They share a common objective: to exploit a host organism's nervous system, altering its behaviour for the parasite's benefit.

Mob Mentality - The Lofty Ambitions of Cordyceps Fungus

Cordyceps are a diverse group of parasitic fungi that have evolved over millions of years. They belong to the *Ascomycota* phylum and are found in ecosystems worldwide, from tropical rainforests to temperate woodlands. Their name, Cordyceps, is derived from the Greek words "kordyle," meaning club, and "kephale," meaning head, owing to the club-shaped fruiting bodies that they produce.

The Parasitic Nature:

What makes Cordyceps truly fascinating is their parasitic lifestyle. These fungi primarily target insects and other arthropods. When a Cordyceps spore lands on a potential host, it infiltrates the body, taking control of its nervous system. The host insect's behaviour becomes manipulated as it is driven to climb to a high point, usually a plant or tree. This bizarre behaviour ensures that when the fungus eventually erupts from the host, it releases its spores from an elevated position, maximising their chances of spreading to new hosts below.

A Symphony of Species:
Cordyceps is not a single species but a vast and diverse group, with over 400 different species identified. Each species displays unique adaptations, specialising in infecting particular insect hosts. For example, *Ophiocordyceps unilateralis* targets ants, while *Cordyceps sinensis* thrives in the bodies of caterpillars. This specialisation reflects the intricacies of coevolution between the fungus and its hosts.
Beyond their remarkable ecological role, some Cordyceps species have gained notoriety for their potential medicinal properties. *Cordyceps sinensis,* also known as "Himalayan Viagra," has been used in traditional Chinese medicine for centuries. It is believed to have various health benefits, from boosting energy levels to improving respiratory function. However, scientific research on the efficacy of Cordyceps as a medicinal fungus remains ongoing.

The Dance of Life and Death:
Cordyceps fungi remind us of the eternal cycle of life and death in the natural world. While they may seem like harbingers of doom for their insect hosts, they play an essential role in regulating insect populations, preventing overpopulation that could harm ecosystems.
In the enigmatic world of Cordyceps, the line between life and death is a thin one, where parasitism and adaptation merge into a mesmerising dance.

Man's Best Friend - The Hijacking Antics of *Toxoplasma gondii*

Toxoplasma gondii is a member of the phylum *Apicomplexa* and is responsible for a disease called toxoplasmosis. It is estimated that up to a third of the world's human population has been exposed to this parasite at some point in their lives. The primary host for *T. gondii* is the domestic cat, where the parasite can complete its complex life cycle.

The Ingenious Life Cycle:

The life cycle of *T. gondii* is a testament to its adaptability. It begins when oocysts, containing the infectious form of the parasite, are shed in the cat's feces. These oocysts can survive in the environment for months, posing a risk to other animals that come into contact with contaminated soil or water.
One of the most intriguing aspects of *T. gondii* is its ability to manipulate the behaviour of its intermediate hosts, which can include rodents, birds, and even humans. Studies have shown that infected rodents lose their natural aversion to the scent of cat urine, making them more likely to be eaten by a cat, thereby completing the parasite's life cycle. In humans, the effects are subtler but still present, with some studies suggesting potential links between *T. gondii* infection and changes in behaviour, such as increased risk-taking and alterations in personality.

A Stealthy Intruder:

Toxoplasma gondii is known for its ability to evade the host's immune system by forming cysts in various tissues, including the brain. These cysts can remain dormant for years, making the parasite a lifelong companion for its host. While most healthy individuals may not experience severe symptoms from *T. gondii* infection, it can pose a significant risk to people with compromised immune systems and pregnant women.

Research into *Toxoplasma gondii* continues to unveil its complexities and the extent of its influence on both animal and human behaviour.

The Puppeteer's Strings - The Hairworm

Hairworms begin their lives as tiny, worm-like larvae in freshwater habitats such as ponds, streams, and rivers. Here, they feed on small organisms, developing into long, hair-thin worms, often reaching lengths of up to several feet. These aquatic larvae may seem unremarkable, but their transformation into parasitic adults is anything but ordinary.

A Mysterious Metamorphosis:
When it's time to reproduce, hairworms undergo a remarkable transformation. They stop feeding, becoming entirely dependent on their stored energy reserves. At this stage, they leave the safety of the water and seek out terrestrial environments, often climbing onto vegetation near the water's edge.

The Insect Hosts:
The next chapter of the hairworm's life is both gruesome and ingenious. They manipulate unwitting insects, typically grasshoppers, crickets, or mantises, into becoming their involuntary hosts. The adult hairworm secretes chemicals that influence the host's nervous system, compelling it to jump into water. Once submerged, the hairworm exits the host, leaving it to drown while the parasite swims away freely.
As hairworms return to the water, they engage in a frenzied quest to find a mate. Once the mating is complete, the female hairworm lays her eggs, and the cycle begins anew. This peculiar life cycle represents an intricate balance between nature's forces, where hairworms exploit both aquatic and terrestrial environments to perpetuate their species.

Mysteries and Marvels:
Despite their bizarre lifestyle, hairworms remain relatively mysterious to scientists, and many questions about their physiology and behaviour remain unanswered.

An Unassuming Mastermind - The Lancet Liver Fluke

The Lancet Liver Fluke begins its life as an egg, typically laid in the liver of a mammalian host, such as a cow, sheep, or deer. Once hatched, the larvae migrate into the host's liver tissue, where they develop into mature flukes.

An Ingenious Journey:

Here's where the Lancet Liver Fluke's story takes a devious turn. These adult flukes produce tiny, sac-like structures filled with eggs. These sacs are then excreted by the host through its bile ducts and eventually end up in the host's feces.

The next step in this parasitic saga involves a secondary host—a snail. The eggs in the sacs hatch into larvae when they come into contact with water, such as rain or dew. These larvae are ingested by snails, where they develop further and multiply.

This is where the Lancet Liver Fluke's manipulative prowess takes centre stage. The larvae leave the snail in a form known as cercariae and take on an aquatic lifestyle. But they don't stop there. These tiny creatures are programmed to seek out and enter the body of an unsuspecting ant.

Mind Control Unleashed:

Once inside the ant, the Lancet Liver Fluke larvae engage in a form of mind control. They migrate to the ant's brain and secrete chemicals that alter the ant's behaviour. Infected ants become more active and are drawn to the tops of grass blades, making them more likely to be consumed by grazing mammals. When the infected ant is eaten by a mammal, the cycle comes full circle. The Lancet Liver Fluke larvae enter the mammal's liver, develop into adults, and the process repeats itself.

The Lancet Liver Fluke's life cycle is a testament to the intricacies of parasitic relationships in the natural world. It showcases how parasites have evolved remarkable adaptations to exploit multiple hosts and ensure their own survival.

A Beautiful Nightmare - The Emerald Cockroach Wasp

In the world of entomology, few creatures exhibit the precision and sophistication of the Emerald Cockroach Wasp, also known by its scientific name Ampulex compressa. This tiny wasp, no larger than a paperclip, possesses a remarkable and chilling ability to transform a cockroach into a zombie-like servant, ensuring its offspring's survival in a gruesome yet awe-inspiring spectacle.

A Delicate Yet Deadly Predator:

The Emerald Cockroach Wasp's striking emerald-green and iridescent body belies its sinister purpose. It is a parasitoid, meaning it relies on another organism for its reproduction. Its target: the American cockroach. The wasp's modus operandi is a precise and intricate ritual. It starts by locating a cockroach, typically one that is larger and stronger than itself. The wasp delivers a sting to the cockroach's thorax, injecting a venom that temporarily paralyses the roach's front legs.

Zombification Begins:

With the cockroach immobilised but still alive, the wasp leads it to its underground lair. There, the wasp lays an egg on the cockroach's abdomen and seals it inside a burrow. As the larva hatches, it feeds on the still-living cockroach's body, consuming it methodically to ensure its own growth. What truly sets the Emerald Cockroach Wasp apart is its ability to manipulate the behaviour of the cockroach. The venom not only paralyses the roach but also alters its neural circuits. As a result, the cockroach becomes docile and complies with the wasp's commands.

A Morbid Partnership:

The cockroach, now a submissive pawn in the wasp's game, remains alive as the larva consumes its non-essential organs. It ensures the cockroach stays fresh and provides sustenance throughout its development. Once the larva has grown and pupated, it emerges from the cockroach's body as a fully developed wasp. The cycle repeats, with the wasp continuing its search for another cockroach victim to ensure the survival of its offspring.

Unconventional Deluges - The Curious World of Non-Water Floods

The Sticky Situation: The Great Molasses Flood of 1919

Picture this: it's a warm day in Boston, Massachusetts, and suddenly, you find yourself waist-deep in a tsunami of molasses. Yes, molasses—the same sticky stuff you might put on pancakes.

A Sweet Business Decision

Our story begins with the Purity Distilling Company, which decided it was a brilliant idea to store over two million gallons of molasses in a massive tank in Boston's North End. This was during the era of Prohibition, mind you, so perhaps they thought they could brew up a sweet underground operation. Little did they know that the tank was a ticking time bomb. It was poorly constructed, and people had reportedly heard strange creaking and groaning noises coming from it. But hey, who would've thought a tank of molasses could be dangerous, right?

January 15, 1919: Molasses Madness

On this fateful day, with the temperature rising and fermentation doing its thing, the tank burst open like the Kool-Aid Man crashing through a wall, but instead of saying "Oh yeah!" it unleashed a tidal wave of molasses, racing through the streets at an astonishing 35 miles per hour. Talk about a molasses speed run!

This sugary tsunami demolished everything in its path. Houses crumbled, a firehouse was knocked off its foundation (the irony!), and people found themselves trapped in the gooey mess. Imagine trying to run from an advancing wall of molasses—it's not as sweet as it sounds.

Sweet Tragedy

The disaster left 21 people dead and 150 injured, not to mention countless horses and dogs succumbed to the molasses maelstrom. Cleanup was a mess (literally and figuratively) and took months. They say you could still smell molasses on hot summer days years later.

Legal battles ensued, with the Purity Distilling Company facing a sticky situation of their own. They were held responsible for the disaster and had to pay settlements to the victims. As for the tank, well, it's safe to say they didn't build another one.

So, the next time you pour some molasses on your pancakes, remember the molasses wave that shook Boston, and savour the sticky history that accompanies this sweet condiment.

The Salty Slip-Up: The Great Boston Brine Spill of 1919

Move over molasses, there's a new liquid disaster in town, and it's salty! In 1919, the city of Boston experienced an incident so peculiar that it left residents both amused and perplexed–the Great Boston Brine Spill. Let's dive into the salty saga of how a simple error turned into a pickle of a problem.

A Slip of the Valve

Our story begins at a warehouse in East Cambridge, where workers were diligently operating massive tanks filled with–you guessed it–brine. For those not in the know, brine is basically water that's been soaking in salt's company for a while, and it's often used for pickling and preserving food.

On this fine day in 1919, a worker intended to open a valve but mistakenly closed it instead. You might think this isn't a big dill (pun intended), but consider this: the tank held 2.3 million gallons of brine. So, when that valve was reopened, chaos ensued.

Brine, Brine, Everywhere

With the valve reopened, the warehouse floor became a briny slip 'n slide. Millions of gallons of brine gushed out, flooding the surrounding streets and even making its way into nearby homes. Imagine trying to explain to your neighbour why your living room is suddenly a pickle paradise.

The brine continued its relentless flow for hours, creating a mess that turned streets into salty rivers and sidewalks into treacherous salt flats. Bostonians watched in amazement as their city was seasoned to perfection.

Pickled Pavement

Cleaning up the mess was no small feat. It took days to pump out the brine and weeks to remove the salt deposits from the streets. People reportedly walked on salted sidewalks as if they were strolling through a snow-covered landscape.
Despite the inconvenience, Bostonians had a sense of humour about the whole ordeal. Jokes about the "Pickle Parade" and "Salty Streets" circulated, and some even took the opportunity to lay down a few puns that would make a dad proud.

The Great Boston Brine Spill of 1919 reminds us that history sometimes serves up stories so unusual, you'd think they were marinated in comedy. But no, this was a real pickle, or rather, a real brine situation.

Ale Armageddon: The London Beer Flood of 1814

It was a dark and stormy night in London, and what began as a regular day at the Meux and Company Brewery would soon turn into a tale as frothy as the beer they brewed. Welcome to the London Beer Flood of 1814, a sudsy catastrophe that left a lasting mark on the city's history and a few beer-soaked stories to toast to.

A Vast Sea of Beer

Our story begins at the Horse Shoe Brewery in London's Tottenham Court Road, where vast quantities of beer were brewed, stored, and fermented in gigantic vats. And when we say vast, we're talking about some of the largest beer tanks in the world, holding tens of thousands of barrels each.

A Fermentation Fiasco

On October 17, 1814, one of these massive vats couldn't handle the pressure. Its iron bands snapped with a thunderous roar, and a tidal wave of beer, 135,000 gallons of it, was unleashed.

A Wave of Hoppiness

The released beer surged through the brewery like a boozy tsunami, sweeping away everything in its path. Buildings were demolished, and streets were flooded with a river of ale. Imagine watching your cozy London neighbourhood turn into a sea of suds. Talk about a beer bath!

In the aftermath, brave souls and bystanders reportedly scrambled to scoop up the beer with pots, pans, and even their own hands. In a scene that sounds like a pub crawl gone wild, people filled their containers with the free-flowing ale. Hey, who could blame them?

Drunk in the Streets

Cleaning up the mess took weeks, and the area around the brewery reportedly smelled like a pub that never closed. Some accounts even suggest that local residents complained about the overpowering smell of beer in their homes.

The brewery's owners, perhaps not thrilled about losing all that precious beer, took legal action. However, the court ruled that the disaster was an "Act of God," absolving the brewery of liability. To this day, it remains one of the most divine excuses for a beer flood.

Nautical Curiosities - Mysteries of the Abyss

Whether it's the seemingly endless horizons, the chilling silence, or the endless depths; the ocean has remained a source of constant fear and fascination for humanity since time immemorial. Whatever the reason, or the emotions it elicits, the sea houses almost as many enigmas as it does fish.

An Endless Holiday - The Disappearances of the Bermuda Triangle

The Bermuda Triangle is not the typical locale for a cradle of terror. Nestled between the tropical havens of Miami, Bermuda, and Puerto Rico, the vast expanse of the triangle has long remained the centre of a centuries old mystery. Numerous accounts attest to the unsolved disappearances of almost anything that passes through the unusual area. Ships, planes, submarines, even dinghies; nothing is safe.

An Age-Old Mystery

The first known disappearance, directly attributed to the triangle, was of an American armed vessel. Commissioned in 1798, the USS *Pickering,* a 'topsail schooner', was designed to combat the French occupation of Guadeloupe. By 1800, the vessel had earned a reputation as a reliable fighter, and extraordinarily fast traveller, due to its success in a military campaign against French mercenaries and it's daring rescue of the USS *Portland.* Subsequently, in June of the same year, the *Pickering* set off a peacekeeping mission from Boston to Guadeloupe. The ship was last seen off the coast of Delaware. Whilst passing through the Bermuda Triangle, the entirety of the ship and its 91 member crew, simply vanished into thin air. Theories at the time believed that the boat may have been lost in a gale, yet no contemporary records exist of strong enough winds to have destroyed a military vessel.
Likewise, unsolved disappearances of aircraft have occurred within the area almost since they first traversed the area. The

first documented missing aircraft over the Bermuda Triangle was that of the now infamous 'General Motors Flight 19'. On December 5th 1945, the U.S. Navy was conducting an 'open air exercise', wherein a small designation of 5 TPM Avenger Torpedo Bombers, led by one Lieutenant Charles Taylor, were practicing the use of precise navigational technology. Only halfway through the session, all 5 aircraft lost contact with their base of operations, leading to the dispatch of a Martin PBM Mariner, in an attempted retrieval operation. All 6 aircraft - along with the total crew of 27 - vanished in the same area and have never been recovered.

Among the more peculiar aspects of each incident has been the conspicuous absence of any forewarning. No-SOS signals, no distress signals, no survivors, no wrecks. It's as if each craft and it's crew has simply vanished into thin air.

The Blame Game

There are perhaps more theories regarding the true nature of the 'Devil's Gateway' than there are missing ships within it! So devoid of evidence and answers are the strange vanishing acts that many proposed causes have jumped to outlandish conclusions; though that's not to say they don't possess at least a modicum of truth.

Proposed in the paranoia-fuelled UFO frenzy of the 1960's, some have suggested that the site of the triangle bears some special significance to extraterrestrial beings, and that the arrival of manned vessels in the region has unwittingly drawn their cosmic ire. Perhaps stranger still is the belief of some that the triangle is in fact a wormhole, or portal, to alternate dimension; a bridge between realities.

One can only imagine blacking out behind the rudder of a merchant vessel, before waking up in the laboratory of an extra-dimensional entity.

Magnets and Brimstone

Among the more scientific explanations for the strange phenomena in the area are magnetic anomalies, and methane hydrate eruptions. Both theories hinge on the fact that Bermuda Triangle happens to lay at the convergence point of multiple tectonic plates. As such, chemical processes beneath the surface of the ocean could produce large, pressurised pockets of methane hydrate gas, which erupt when disturbed. It's not too hard to imagine an old galleon weighing anchor near the shores of a small remote island, only to accidentally snag a deathly trap on the sea floor. Similarly, the constant flow of molten magnetic materials could result in the seemingly demonic triangle actually being home to little more than bizarre magnetic anomalies, which disrupt the otherwise infallible navigational systems of modern vehicles.

Whatever the case may be, the next time you find yourself yearning for a tropical getaway, keep a close eye on your rubber ducky. You never know where it might end up.

Japan's Extraterrestrial Enigma - Subaquatic Crop Circles

Amami Ōshima is a small island located in Japan's beautiful Ryukyu Island Archipelago. The island is sparsely populated, but bears a long, rich cultural heritage, having been inhabited for thousands of years. Beside it's ancient population, and scenic shorelines, the island is largely unremarkable. Accordingly, it came as quite the shock to the island when, in 1995, a team of wildlife researchers found a large number of exceedingly bizarre, ornate sculptures in the waters lining the southern coast. The confounding constructs were each constructed of perfectly symmetrical, concentric geometric circles. The precision of the strokes used to carve out the structures was extraordinary and indicated to researchers that whatever was behind these coastal crop circles possessed incredible intellect.

Love and Monsters

Early theories began to emerge from locals, and sensationalised accounts further afield, that perhaps mythical beings were behind the structures. Some proposed that the legendary Japanese creatures, known as Kappa, were responsible for the unusual crop circles. According to folklore, the Kappa was a turtle-like monster with a cavernous head filled with water.
In 2012, an equally outlandish, but demonstrably true reason was discovered. The constructive culprits were found to be a previously undiscovered species of pufferfish. Named *Torquigener albomaculosus*, the rather innocuous looking fish is possessed of incredible artistic prowess. Unbelievably, in the years since the shocking discovery, much has been learnt of the clever little fish. The males of the species use their limbs, mouths, and hand (or fin) made tools to carve out their very own uniquely designed geometrically inspired nests, which help them to attract and communicate with potentially mates. Females seek out the nests that they find most attractive and appear to even draw meaning from the artwork of potential

partners. In essence, each of the pufferfish's sea floor sculptures is a heartfelt love letter to their kind.

Whilst perhaps not as scintillating as a maleficent turtle demon, the inspiring creativity of *T. albomaculosus* ought to serve as a reminder never to underestimate, or under value, even the most inconspicuous of beings.

A Cold Water Cacophony- The Bloop

This enigmatic auditory event, akin to an otherworldly underwater belch, sent shockwaves through the scientific community and sparked wild speculations about its origins.

A Sonic Enigma

Our story begins in the vast expanse of the Pacific Ocean, where the ocean's depths hide secrets that have eluded human discovery for centuries. In the late 20th century, a series of underwater microphones, known as hydrophones, were placed strategically to monitor and record the sounds of the deep. These hydrophones were part of the U.S. Navy's Sound Surveillance System (SOSUS), designed to track submarines during the Cold War. Little did they know that one day, these sensitive instruments would pick up a sound so peculiar, it would defy conventional explanation.

July 11, 1997, on this fateful day, a hydrophone located in the Equatorial Pacific Ocean, about 3,000 miles (4,800 kilometers) west of the coast of South America, recorded something that would later become famous as the Bloop sound. To describe it simply, the Bloop sounded like a colossal underwater roar—a deep and powerful sound that resonated for several minutes. For context, imagine the sound of a large shipping vessel passing by, amplified a thousandfold, and you're in the ballpark of the Bloop. It was a sonic event so massive that it dwarfed any previously recorded underwater noise, including the vocalisations of the largest whales. To put it in perspective, it was roughly 16 times louder than the call of the blue whale, the largest animal on Earth.

Wild Speculations

As soon as scientists at the National Oceanic and Atmospheric Administration (NOAA) heard the recording, they knew they had stumbled upon something extraordinary. The Bloop was unlike anything they had encountered before. Its sheer volume and the duration of the sound were baffling.

In the spirit of scientific inquiry, the race was on to decipher the source of this enigmatic noise. As news of the Bloop sound spread, it captured the collective imagination of the public, leading to a slew of wild speculations and theories. Here are some of the most imaginative ones:

The Kraken's Roar

The maritime world has long been fertile ground for myths and legends, and few creatures capture the human imagination like the Kraken—a mythical sea monster with tentacles capable of ensnaring entire ships. Naturally, when confronted with an unexplained underwater noise of epic proportions, some couldn't resist the temptation to evoke the Kraken.

According to this theory, the Bloop was the deafening roar of the Kraken, awakening from its deep-sea slumber. It was a tantalising notion—the idea that such a creature might exist in the uncharted depths, lurking just beyond our understanding. Of course, scientists and marine biologists were quick to point out that there was no concrete evidence supporting the existence of such a colossal cephalopod. The Kraken, while a fascinating legend, remained firmly in the realm of mythology.

Secret Military Experiments

Conspiracy theorists, always ready to weave tales of shadowy government operations, were quick to suggest that the Bloop was the result of top-secret military experiments. Some believed it was the sonic signature of an advanced submarine or underwater weapon system.

While it's true that governments around the world have conducted classified experiments in the ocean, there was no credible evidence linking the Bloop to any covert military activities. The theory remained speculative at best, lacking concrete proof.

Underwater Volcanic Eruptions

Volcanoes, both on land and under the sea, are notorious for their explosive eruptions and the release of tremendous energy. Some scientists speculated that the Bloop might be the result of an underwater volcanic eruption, with the sound echoing through the oceanic depths.

This theory seemed plausible at first glance, given the seismic activity in the Earth's crust and the fact that underwater volcanic eruptions can indeed produce loud noises. However, further investigation revealed no corresponding volcanic activity in the region at the time of the Bloop sound. The volcanic theory, while a valid scientific explanation for some underwater noises, fell short in this case.

Massive Unidentified Sea Creature

Perhaps the most tantalising theory of all was the suggestion that the Bloop was the vocalisation of a colossal, undiscovered sea creature. Imaginations ran wild with visions of sea serpents or Leviathan-like beings dwelling in the darkest depths of the ocean.

While the prospect of discovering a new species with the power to produce such a sound was undeniably exciting, it presented its own set of challenges. The oceans are vast and largely unexplored, making it difficult to substantiate claims of undiscovered mega-fauna. Moreover, the source of the sound seemed to move, making it unlikely to be a stationary creature.

The Real Culprit Unmasked

As theories about the Bloop swirled, scientists at NOAA were determined to get to the bottom of the mystery. They knew that solving the puzzle required meticulous investigation and a comprehensive understanding of underwater acoustics.

In 2005, the truth behind the Bloop sound was finally revealed, and it wasn't the stuff of legends or conspiracy theories. It was a natural phenomenon, both fascinating and humbling in its simplicity: the Bloop was the sound of icebergs breaking apart and calving in the frigid waters of Antarctica.

Iceberg calving, the process by which large chunks of ice detach from glaciers and ice shelves, can generate tremendous acoustic events. When these massive icebergs fracture and tumble into the ocean, they release a burst of sound energy that reverberates through the water.

In the case of the Bloop, the source of the sound was identified as a particularly large and distant iceberg undergoing an immense calving event. The sound, produced by the fracture and separation of ice, traveled thousands of miles through the ocean, eventually reaching the Equatorial Pacific, where it was recorded by the hydrophone.

"There's magic in the water that draws all men away from the land..."
- Herman Melville

Beasts that Beggar Belief - A Bizarre Bestiary

In the manner of a mighty dynasty, humans have conquered Earth emphatically. Accordingly, it is easy, and often desirable, for us as a species to forget that we share our collective home with myriad creatures; from the murky trenches of the ocean, all the way to the cloud-piercing claws of mountaintops, we are surrounded by creatures that challenge our perception of reality.

Baby Dragons - The Olm

Deep within the caves of the Balkans, there exists an extraordinary network of hidden subterranean rivers; sprawling like a colossal cobweb beneath the earth's surface. Many centuries ago, when Slovenian and Italian farmers chanced upon these great cavernous waters, they found themselves face to face with a most unusual creature. Tucked away in the murky depths was a thriving population of minuscule silver serpents; unfathomable in their apparent simplicity. The Balkan people, both astounded and horrified by these fleshy wyrms, believed them to be the concealed offspring of dragons from a far-off land. Not wanting to draw the ire of their fire-breathing mother, the 'baby dragons' were left unperturbed for millennia, and the legend of the Olm was born. The subsequent study and revelations of the olm (*Proteus anguinus*) are perhaps even more incredible than the legend of their origins.

Preternatural Properties

The olm is a cave-dwelling, aquatic amphibian, reminiscent to a salamander. Only 8 inches in length, the olm possesses no pigment in its skin, giving it a distinctive glassy exterior. Its eyes are covered in this pink flesh, rendering it almost completely blind, however, these eyes have been observed to regrow, when the olm is exposed to light for a prolonged period of the time. The baby dragons possess heightened senses underwater, such as incredible olfactory perceptions, and a bizarre ability to detect the electrical fields produced by other organisms.

Never-Ending Story

Among the more unusual features of the olm is it's practical immortality. These strange creatures are born as 'feathery' gilled larvae, and gradually become smoother and larger as they grow. The species has been observed to live in excess of hundreds of years, and is even capable of regenerating entire limbs and organs. Remarkably, some olms have displayed the seemingly supernatural ability to regrow portions of their brain, complete with it's associated memories and functions. Astonishingly, the olm is able to accomplish these feats of unbelievable longevity whilst also sustaining itself on no more than a morsel of food every few years.

The Fountain of Youth - The Immortal Jellyfish

In the enigmatic depths of the world's oceans, where the blue abyss stretches as far as the eye can see, an incredible phenomenon unfolds—a creature defying the very concept of aging. Meet the immortal jellyfish, a remarkable marine species that has earned its moniker by exhibiting a remarkable ability to revert its biological clock and essentially become ageless.

A Journey Through Time

Imagine a creature that experiences aging in reverse, a biological Benjamin Button of the sea. The immortal jellyfish (*Turritopsis dohrnii*) possesses the extraordinary capability to transform from an adult jellyfish back to its juvenile stage, effectively resetting its biological clock. This unique feature is at the heart of its intriguing moniker, the "immortal" jellyfish.
The key to the immortal jellyfish's remarkable ability lies in its process of transdifferentiation. When faced with unfavourable conditions or stressors, these jellyfish can revert their specialised cells back to a more primitive state, effectively erasing the effects of aging and rejuvenating themselves. This remarkable regenerative power allows them to transform their body tissues into a younger form.
The habitat of the immortal jellyfish spans across oceans worldwide, with notable populations found in the Mediterranean Sea, the waters off Japan, and the Caribbean. These translucent jellyfish drift with ocean currents, making them difficult to spot in their natural environment.

A Tiny and Delicate Wonder

Among the diverse species of jellyfish, the immortal jellyfish is relatively small, measuring only about 4.5 millimetres in diameter when fully grown. Its diminutive size belies its incredible regenerative abilities.

The life cycle of the immortal jellyfish is a story of transformation and renewal. It begins as a tiny larva, known as a planula, which attaches itself to a solid surface, like a rock or the sea floor, and metamorphoses into a polyp. This polyp grows into a colony of jellyfish, called a hydroid, with specialised feeding and reproductive individuals. However, when faced with adverse conditions or damage, the hydroid can undergo transdifferentiation, reverting its cells and forming medusae–the adult jellyfish.

The most astonishing phase of the immortal jellyfish's life cycle is the transition from medusa to polyp, effectively reversing the aging process. Instead of dying, the jellyfish becomes younger, transforming back into the juvenile stage and starting the cycle anew. This biological marvel is what earned it the nickname "immortal."

The rejuvenation of the immortal jellyfish is not a one-time event but a continuous cycle. In favourable conditions, they can grow into mature medusae, reproduce, and then, when environmental stressors or aging sets in, revert to their juvenile state once again. This perpetual renewal process ensures that they can potentially evade death from old age.

A Window Into Aging

The immortal jellyfish has captured the attention of scientists and researchers around the world for its unique ability to defy aging. It offers a glimpse into the biological mechanisms that underlie the aging process, particularly the potential for cellular rejuvenation and tissue regeneration.

The study of the immortal jellyfish has significant implications for regenerative medicine. Understanding the genetic and cellular processes that allow these jellyfish to reverse their aging could inspire advancements in tissue repair and regeneration in humans.

Marine Masquerade - The Mimic Octopus

Lurking below the seas, where all manner of strange creatures spend their days in a dance of death, there exists one singular champion of this morbid masquerade: the mimic octopus (*Thaumoctopus mimicus*).

Master of Disguise

The mimic octopus owes its name to its uncanny ability to seemingly shape-shift into almost any underwater occupant. It especially favours mimicking unsightly and venomous beings; capable of changing the colour, texture, and shape of its whole body. Some have even been witnessed utilising props and tools to assist in their disguises - scooping up shells and contorting their tentacles to morph into a mass of barnacles or a solitary coral.

Rebels Without a Cause

Mimic octopuses have displayed intelligence that defies their invertebrate nature. Many have demonstrated an aptitude for complex problem solving, such as navigating novel mazes, and assembling puzzles. Additionally, they even appear to grow frustrated if they fail in their intellectual escapades, sometimes lashing out at passing fish to defuse.

This remarkable beast lives for only 2 - 3 years, though they always try to go out in style. Female *T. mimicus* will lay a batch of thousands of eggs, which they gently lay down beside and nurture until they pass away.

Tiny Titans - The Tardigrade

Imagine a creature so small it can fit on the head of a pin, yet possesses a remarkable set of superpowers. Tardigrades, scientifically known as phylum *Tardigrada*, are true survivors of the microcosmos, measuring less than 1.5 millimetres in length but packing a punch in terms of resilience. The name "tardigrade" translates to "slow stepper," which may seem ironic given their reputation for toughness. This name was coined in the 18th century when scientists observed their sluggish movements under microscopes.

Extraordinary Resilience

Tardigrades are famed for their ability to survive in some of the harshest conditions on Earth. They can endure extreme temperatures, from near absolute zero to boiling water, and withstand pressures six times greater than those found in the deepest ocean trenches. Radiation exposure that would be fatal to most life forms barely fazes them. At the heart of their resilience is a remarkable strategy called cryptobiosis. When faced with harsh conditions, tardigrades dehydrate themselves, effectively shutting down their metabolism and turning into a nearly indestructible state. When conditions improve, they rehydrate and come back to life, as if nothing happened.

Global Nomads

Tardigrades are cosmopolitan creatures, found on every continent, from the highest mountain peaks to the deepest ocean trenches. They've even been discovered in some of the most extreme environments on Earth, such as hot springs, Antarctica, and the Sahara Desert. Their ability to survive in such diverse environments makes tardigrades true masters of adaptation and survival. They're often found in moist habitats, including mosses, lichens, leaf litter, and soil.

Beyond Survival

Tardigrades have sparked scientific curiosity beyond their resilience. Researchers are exploring their unique proteins and genetics to develop applications in fields such as cryopreservation, regenerative medicine, and space exploration. Tardigrades play a crucial role in their ecosystems by breaking down organic matter and recycling nutrients. They are essential cogs in the intricate machinery of the microscopic world.

Micro Marvels - The Myxomycetes

In the world of microorganisms, where the line between plant, animal, and fungus blurs, there exists an extraordinary group of organisms known as myxomycetes, or simply slime moulds. These enigmatic life forms are neither plant nor animal nor fungus, and their peculiar biology has fascinated scientists for centuries.

Unearthly Appearance

Picture a vibrant, gelatinous mass that seems to ooze and pulsate across decaying logs and forest floors. This is the curious form of myxomycetes, which have puzzled naturalists and scientists for centuries due to their bizarre, seemingly otherworldly appearance. Myxomycetes belong to a kingdom of life called protists, which is a diverse and often puzzling group. They are neither plants, animals, nor fungi but exist in a category of their own.

Myxomycetes have a dual life cycle that alternates between a mobile, amoeba-like stage and a fruiting body stage. The mobile stage, called a plasmodium, consists of a mass of protoplasm that creeps and engulfs food sources in its path.

The Peculiar Fruiting Body

When conditions become unfavourable, the plasmodium transforms into a fruiting body, often taking on vibrant colours and intricate shapes. These fruiting bodies, known as sporangia, are the reproductive phase of the slime mould. While myxomycetes are typically small and inconspicuous, their fungal cousins, like the honey fungus (*Armillaria*), can reach enormous sizes. The largest living organism on Earth is believed to be an *Armillaria* fungus in Oregon, covering an area of over 2,385 acres!

Inside the sporangia, thousands of spores develop. When the time is right, the sporangia burst open, releasing spores into the environment. These spores can be carried by the wind or hitch rides on passing creatures, aiding in the dispersion of myxomycetes.

Nature's Decomposers

Myxomycetes play a crucial role in ecosystems as decomposers. They break down dead plant material, contributing to the recycling of nutrients and the enrichment of soil. The presence and abundance of myxomycetes can serve as indicators of habitat health and biodiversity, making them valuable to ecological studies and conservation efforts.

Cellular Mysteries

Myxomycetes are of particular interest to scientists studying cell biology and genetics. Their peculiar biology challenges our understanding of how organisms function at the cellular level. Despite their small size and inconspicuous appearance, myxomycetes boast an astonishing diversity of species, with new discoveries still being made. Each species offers a unique window into the intricacies of nature.

Chapter Three

The Strangest of Folk

The Man in the Iron Mask - A Masked Mystery

A character shrouded in secrecy, wrapped in intrigue, and, of course, encased in iron!

A Masked Guest

Our story begins in 17th-century France, a time when elaborate wigs and frilly collars were all the rage. Amid the opulence of the court of King Louis XIV, a mysterious guest arrived at the Bastille, a notorious prison in Paris. The catch? He was donning a mask made of iron, and no one knew his true identity.

The Man in the Iron Mask was a living riddle, a puzzle that would baffle historians, philosophers, and conspiracy theorists for centuries to come. But let's not get ahead of ourselves; the Man in the Iron Mask was far from your typical prisoner.

Fashionable Prisonwear

Picture this: a man wearing the latest in 17th-century fashion—except for the fact that his head was enclosed in a solid iron mask! Rumour had it that the mask was so heavy that he had to be fed through a small opening, like some medieval astronaut with a penchant for French couture.

Why the mask, you ask? Ah, dear reader, that's where the plot thickens. The mask was meant to conceal the Man's identity, leaving him not only unable to speak but also utterly anonymous. Was he a disgraced noble? A spy? A secret twin of the king himself? The possibilities were as numerous as the wigs in Versailles.

The Plot Thickens

As the years rolled by, the enigma of the Man in the Iron Mask deepened. His identity was kept under tight wraps, leading to wild speculations and conspiracy theories. Theories ranged from the plausible to the downright fantastical.

Some believed he was the rightful heir to the French throne, a twin brother of Louis XIV separated at birth. Others suspected he held dangerous state secrets that could topple the monarchy. And, of course, there were those who insisted he was a time-traveling astronaut stuck in the wrong century.

The Masked Musketeer

The legend of the Man in the Iron Mask gained further traction thanks to a certain swashbuckling novelist named Alexandre Dumas. In his novel "The Vicomte of Bragelonne: Ten Years Later," Dumas spun a thrilling tale of political intrigue and masked adventurers.

Dumas' fictionalised account featured none other than the Three Musketeers themselves—Athos, Porthos, and Aramis—on a mission to uncover the identity of the Man in the Iron Mask. It was a rollicking adventure that blended fact and fiction, and it firmly cemented the Man's place in popular culture.

The Real Man Behind the Mask

Now, let's peel away the layers of mystery and unveil the truth about the Man in the Iron Mask. Drumroll, please... He was, drumroll again... A high-ranking, but rather ordinary, prisoner named Eustache Dauger!

Yes, you read that correctly. After decades of speculation, historical sleuths uncovered documents that revealed the Man's true identity. Eustache Dauger was a former valet who had served various French nobles and was imprisoned for reasons that, while not entirely clear, were far from the sensational conspiracies that had swirled around him.

Masked for Posterity

So, why the iron mask, you may wonder? Well, that's where our tale takes an ironic twist. The iron mask, it turns out, was more of a precaution than a punishment. You see, Dauger had

been privy to sensitive information during his years of service, and the French authorities were understandably concerned that he might spill the beans.
Hence, the mask. It was a clever way to keep his lips sealed, even if it made him look like an extra from a low-budget medieval sci-fi flick. Imagine trying to spill state secrets while sounding like a distant relative of Darth Vader. Not very effective, right?

The End of an Enigma
As history would have it, Eustache Dauger lived out his days in relative obscurity, masked and forgotten by all but a few. The enigma of the Man in the Iron Mask, while entertaining, ultimately had a rather mundane resolution.
But fear not, dear reader! The legend of the Man in the Iron Mask endures as a testament to the power of mystery and imagination. It reminds us that history is not just a collection of dates and facts but a treasure trove of stories that can be as thrilling as any work of fiction.

The Irony of Irony
In a final twist of irony, the Man in the Iron Mask remains a celebrated figure in popular culture, perpetuating the very myths that shrouded his identity for centuries. From novels to movies, his story continues to captivate the hearts and minds of storytellers and audiences alike.
So, the next time you don your favourite face mask for a trip to the grocery store, spare a thought for Eustache Dauger, the original masked man of mystery. And remember, whether it's history or fashion, sometimes the best stories are the ones with a dash of wit, a pinch of irony, and just a touch of iron.

Tarrare - The Man with an Insatiable Appetite

The Birth of Tarrare

Tarrare was born in rural France in the late 18th century, the exact date lost to history. Even as a child, he displayed a voracious appetite, consuming prodigious amounts of food and often begging for more. His parents, unable to sustain his insatiable hunger, sent him away at a young age.

An Unnatural Appetite

As Tarrare grew, his appetite only intensified. He could eat an entire quarter of beef in a single day, and his hunger knew no bounds. He became a wandering sideshow attraction, earning money by eating live animals, stones, and even corks. Audiences were both fascinated and horrified by his unnatural ability.

Medical Marvel or Monster?

Tarrare's bizarre abilities eventually drew the attention of medical professionals. Dr. Pierre-François Percy, a prominent French military surgeon, took an interest in the young man. Percy's examinations revealed Tarrare's unusual physical characteristics, including a distended abdomen and the ability to stretch his mouth wide enough to swallow a whole apple. Intrigued by Tarrare's potential, Dr. Percy arranged for him to be admitted to a military hospital. During his time there, Tarrare underwent a series of bizarre and often gruesome experiments. He was fed a variety of substances, from live cats to eels, to determine the limits of his consumption. It was a dark and twisted chapter in the history of medical science.

The Espionage of the Insatiable Spy

In an unexpected turn of events, Tarrare's bizarre talents found a new purpose during the tumultuous years of the French

Revolution. He was recruited as a spy by the French military and given a mission that was as audacious as it was strange–to carry a message to a French colonel imprisoned by the Prussians.

Tarrare faced enormous risks on his mission. To avoid capture, he had to swallow a wooden box containing the message. The plan was for him to retrieve the box after passing through enemy lines, but things took an unexpected and stomach-turning turn.

Tarrare's espionage mission ended in tragedy. He was captured by the Prussians, and under suspicion of being a spy, he underwent a brutal interrogation. Despite his suffering, he refused to reveal his mission or betray his country. In the end, he made the ultimate sacrifice for France.

The Tragic End

Tarrare's life came to a mysterious and tragic end. After his release by the Prussians, he returned to France, where his health rapidly deteriorated. His insatiable appetite had taken a toll on his body, and he was plagued by severe infections and constant diarrhoea. So stricken was he by constant hunger that he resorted to eating food waste, live animals, and even... corpses. In 1796, after a local boy went missing from a hospital, suspicion soon grew that Tarrare's appetite had outgrown his sensibilities.

In his final days, Tarrare's condition worsened to the point where he was unable to consume food. He wasted away, his once robust frame reduced to a mere skeleton. On the 17th of June, 1798, Tarrare died in agony, his death shrouded in mystery.

Medical Enigma

Tarrare's life and death have perplexed medical professionals for centuries. What caused his insatiable appetite? Was it a psychological disorder, a physical anomaly, or a combination of both? His bizarre condition remains a subject of debate and fascination among researchers. Some have suggested that Tarrare was a tragic vessel for a number of parasitic worms, whilst others believe he possessed an as of yet unknown syndrome which greatly accelerated his metabolism.

"Hunger knows no friend but it's feeder."
- Aristophanes

Rasputin - Mystic, Confidant, Enigma

Grigori Rasputin, the enigmatic and controversial figure who insinuated himself into the Russian Imperial Court, is a name that continues to evoke fascination and intrigue. His life was shrouded in mysteries, marked by scandals, and tainted by rumours of scandalous affairs. In this detailed account, we will delve into the tumultuous world of Rasputin, exploring the mysteries that surround him, the scandals that defined his reputation, and the affairs that both empowered and endangered him.

The Mystic's Arrival

Rasputin's journey into the inner circles of the Russian court began in the early 20th century when he arrived in Saint Petersburg, claiming to possess mystic and healing powers. His unorthodox methods, often involving fervent prayer and intense hypnotic stares, garnered him the attention of desperate parents, including the Romanovs.

Empress Alexandra, in particular, became an ardent believer in Rasputin's abilities. Her son, Alexei, suffered from haemophilia, a life-threatening condition, wherein sufferers' bodies are incapable of forming life-saving blood clots to assist in the healing of wounds. Rasputin's purported ability to alleviate the boy's pain and stop his bleeding episodes endeared him to the royal family; casting a shadow of holy mystique.

The Scandalous Ascendance

Rasputin's growing influence at court did not go unnoticed. His unkempt appearance, erratic behaviour, and rumoured debaucheries earned him the scorn of the Russian nobility. He was accused of engaging in orgies, indulging in alcohol, and exploiting his connection with the Romanovs for personal gain. Many tales began to sprout of his 12-inch 'man-hood', and near mythic ability to induce both pain and pleasure of epic

proportions. Such tell was not too kindly received by the stuffy aristocracy of the early-20th century.
In 1914, Rasputin was purportedly subject to an assassination attempt when he was lured to a woman's apartment and fed cyanide-laced cakes and wine. To everyone's astonishment, he survived, further fuelling rumours of his supernatural powers. Subsequently, his defiance of death only served to further his political influence.

The Affairs and Intrigues

Rasputin's relationship with Empress Alexandra raised eyebrows and fuelled speculation about an affair. While there is no concrete evidence of a romantic liaison, their intense correspondence and his frequent presence at court fuelled rumours of impropriety.
Rasputin's influence over the Romanovs extended beyond the palace. He had his own group of followers, known as the "Rasputin Girls," who were young women drawn to his charisma and mysticism. The extent of his relationships with these women remains a subject of speculation, though it's safe to say they weren't exactly hanging around for his off-key remarks and zany sense of humour.

The Fall of the House of Romanov

As World War I raged on, Russia faced internal strife and economic hardship. Years of poorly implemented reforms - from the Emancipation of the Serfs in 1861, to the farcical formation of the Duma in 1905 - had ravaged the public's trust in the monolithic Romanov dynasty. Worse still, Rasputin's continued presence at court became a symbol of the monarchy's ineptitude and further eroded public trust in the Romanovs. His dishevelled appearance and supposed preternatural power were frequent talking points of the growing Royalist opposition, with many amongst the largely rural working class regarding him as a "warlock" far more than a healer.

The Plot to Eliminate Rasputin

In December 1916, a group of nobles led by Prince Felix Yusupov hatched a plan to assassinate Rasputin. They lured him to Yusupov's palace, where they poisoned him, using cyanide laced caked and wine. Rasputin, seemingly immune and oblivious to the toxic concoctions with which he was so generously presented, asked for a second helping! In a blind panic, the flustered nobility shot him multiple times. Perhaps unsurprisingly, Rasputin decided that he didn't much care for this offering (he much preferred the bitter almond flavoured cake) and left the gathering early; fleeing to the palace courtyard. Here, the mad monk was captured and bound by the duplicitous aristocrats, before his wounded body was thrown into the icy depths of the Neva River. Some accounts suggest that nobility was so fearful of a potentially vengeful Rasputin coming back to avenge himself, that they sent a servant boy to check for his corpse the following day. Supposedly, there was no sign of the sorcerer, nor his shackles, but the glassy ice that encircled the river was covered in scratch marks, as though a feral beast had clawed its way through. All in all, Rasputin's death marked the end of an era and did little to save the Romanov dynasty.

The Unresolved Mysteries

Rasputin's life and death remain steeped in mysteries and controversies. While his reputation has been coloured by allegations of sexual impropriety and manipulation, his influence over the Romanovs, particularly the Empress, cannot be denied.

Rasputin's story endures as a cautionary tale of the dangers of unchecked influence and the perils of royal privilege, ultimately serving as a reminder of the age old saying "Keep your friends close, and your enemies closer, because you never know what Serbian exiles are up to whilst they're in captivity..."

Caligula - A Reign of Absurdity and Excess

Gaius Julius Caesar Augustus Germanicus, better known as Caligula, took the phrase "absolute power corrupts absolutely" to a whole new level. His reign was a rollercoaster of debauchery, cruelty, and bizarre antics that could rival any modern-day reality TV show. Buckle up, because we're about to take you on a darkly comedic journey through the maddest emperor's outrageous deeds and excessive exploits.

The Kid with Little Boots

Caligula earned his nickname "Caligula," which means "little boots," from the tiny military uniform he wore as a child. Little did anyone know that this seemingly innocent start would lead to a reign of madness.
Caligula's journey to the top began when he was declared emperor at just 24 years old. His ascent was a whirlwind, and as he climbed the ladder of power, he seemed determined to make Rome remember his name, even if it was for all the wrong reasons.

A Circus of Extravagance

Caligula's reign was like one long, never-ending party. He spared no expense when it came to extravagant events, from lavish banquets to wild chariot races. Money was no object, and he was determined to spend it all.
Caligula wasn't content with mere human revelry. He believed that even animals should be part of the party. He hosted grand feasts where he'd dress up his favourite horse, Incitatus, in purple robes and even considered making him a consul. Talk about a horse with political aspirations!

Tyranny, Thy Name Is Caligula

Caligula's sense of humour took a dark turn as he grew in age and power. He became notorious for his cruelty, ordering executions for the slightest offences and playing sadistic mind games with his subjects. It seemed like every day was a game of "Who Will Caligula Offend Today?"

Caligula once hosted a dinner party where he invited dignitaries and had them sit at a table loaded with sumptuous food. The catch? He provided no utensils and watched them struggle to eat. When they complained, he offered them shells as spoons. It was a cruel jest that left his guests torn between laughter and fear.

The Bizarre Bedroom Antics

Caligula had a...let's say, colourful love life. He reportedly had affairs with the wives of senators, engaged in incestuous relationships, and openly flaunted his amorous conquests. No one was safe from his advances, and he showed little regard for traditional Roman morality.

When he got tired of ordinary affairs, Caligula decided to marry not one but three women at the same time. Not in a series of separate ceremonies, mind you, but all at once. Talk about efficiency in matrimonial chaos!

The Maddest End

Caligula's outrageous behaviour eventually caught up with him. A group of senators and members of the Praetorian Guard, the elite military force responsible for guarding the emperor, came together in a plot to eliminate Caligula. They saw his rule as a threat to the stability of the empire and believed that his removal was necessary to save Rome.

The conspirators carefully devised a plan to assassinate Caligula during a series of games held at the Palatine Hill. They knew

the unpredictable emperor would be in attendance, making it an ideal opportunity to strike.
On January 24, AD 41, Caligula attended the games at the Palatine Hill, blissfully unaware of the conspiracy unfolding around him. As he moved through a narrow corridor within the palace, the conspirators sprang into action. Several members of the Praetorian Guard and senators confronted Caligula, attacking him with their concealed weapons. In the chaos that ensued, Caligula was stabbed multiple times, suffering fatal wounds. Caligula's life came to an abrupt and violent end within the palace. He died at the hands of his own guards and trusted senators, who had once sworn allegiance to him. With Caligula's death, a power vacuum emerged in Rome. The Praetorian Guard, responsible for the emperor's safety, played a crucial role in the succession. After a brief period of uncertainty, Caligula's uncle, Claudius, was declared the new emperor.

The Mad Emperor's Legacy

Caligula's reign is a testament to the unpredictable nature of power and the depths of human eccentricity. His legacy endures in countless historical accounts, novels, films, and even adult-themed adaptations that explore the extremes of his infamous exploits.
As we look back on the life of Caligula, we're reminded that history can be as darkly comedic as any farce. His reign was a circus of excess and cruelty, leaving us with stories that make us shake our heads, laugh, and cringe all at once.

"I wish the Roman people had but a single neck!"
- Caligula

Sergei Bryukhonenko and the Autojektor Revolution

Throughout medicine there are individuals whose work transcends the boundaries of their time, forever altering the trajectory of their field. Sergei Bryukhonenko, a brilliant and visionary Soviet scientist, is one such figure. His groundbreaking invention, the Autojektor, ushered in a new era of medical research and has left an indelible mark on the world of life sciences.

The Man Behind the Machine

Sergei Bryukhonenko was born in 1890 in the heart of Russia, a land where the frontiers of science and experimentation held a certain allure. From a young age, he exhibited a profound fascination with the mysteries of life and a relentless curiosity that would shape his career. After completing his education in physiology and medicine, Bryukhonenko embarked on a journey of scientific exploration that would ultimately lead to the creation of the Autojektor.

A Quest for Advancements in Physiology

In the early 20th century, the field of physiology was undergoing a transformation. Scientists were beginning to unlock the intricate workings of the human body, but many questions remained unanswered. Key among these was the challenge of understanding the circulatory system and finding ways to study it outside the living organism.

Bryukhonenko was acutely aware of the limitations of existing research methods. Traditional experiments involving live animals were fraught with ethical concerns and often yielded inconclusive results. Bryukhonenko was driven by the belief that there had to be a better way, a method that would allow researchers to simulate the functions of the circulatory system and observe the vital processes of life without causing harm to living creatures.

The Birth of the Autojektor

Bryukhonenko's vision came to fruition in 1928 when he unveiled the Autojektor, a marvel of engineering and innovation. At its core, the Autojektor was a sophisticated apparatus designed to mimic the functions of the circulatory system. It consisted of a complex network of tubes, pumps, and chambers that could replicate the flow of blood and the exchange of gases within the body.

The Autojektor represented a leap forward in the field of physiology. For the first time, scientists had a tool that could replicate the circulatory processes of a living organism. This revolutionary device allowed researchers to conduct experiments that were previously unthinkable, providing valuable insights into the workings of the human body and the effects of various interventions.

Ethical and Scientific Controversy

While the Autojektor held the promise of advancing medical knowledge and saving countless lives, its creation was not without controversy. The use of live animals, namely decapitated dogs, for the purpose of both experimentation and demonstration drew ire. Some critics questioned the ethical implications of simulating life processes outside a living organism, while others worried about the potential misuse of such technology. Bryukhonenko faced scrutiny and skepticism from some quarters but remained resolute in his pursuit of scientific progress.

Medical Breakthroughs and Advancements

The impact of the Autojektor on medical research was profound. It allowed scientists to study the effects of drugs, surgical techniques, and various medical interventions with unprecedented precision. Researchers could simulate the circulatory responses of patients, making it possible to refine treatment protocols and improve patient outcomes.

One of the most significant breakthroughs facilitated by the Autojektor was the development of cardiopulmonary bypass, a critical component of open-heart surgery. Bryukhonenko's device provided the foundation for this life-saving procedure, which has since saved countless lives around the world.

Legacy and Ethical Considerations

Sergei Bryukhonenko's legacy is a complex one. His invention, the Autojektor, undoubtedly advanced our understanding of physiology and medicine. It paved the way for numerous medical breakthroughs, ultimately improving patient care and outcomes.

However, Bryukhonenko's work also raises important ethical questions that continue to resonate in the world of science and medicine. The ability to simulate life processes outside a living organism challenges our traditional notions of life and death. It forces us to confront the boundaries of ethical experimentation and the responsibilities that come with wielding such powerful technology.

The Autojektor Today

Today, the spirit of innovation that drove Sergei Bryukhonenko lives on. The principles underlying the Autojektor have found new applications in fields such as biomedical engineering and organ transplantation. Devices inspired by Bryukhonenko's work are used to support and sustain patients during critical procedures, pushing the boundaries of what is possible in modern medicine.

Tycho Brahe - The Eccentric Astronomer of the Renaissance

In the winding webs of scientific history, one name stands out as much for its eccentricities as for its groundbreaking discoveries: Tycho Brahe. This 16th-century Danish astronomer defied convention, both in his personal life and his approach to the cosmos, leaving a unique and lasting legacy that continues to inspire astronomers and scholars to this day.

The Man with the Golden Nose

One of the most striking aspects of Tycho Brahe's life was his prosthetic nose. A nobleman by birth, he lost part of his nose in a duel over a mathematical formula. Unwilling to live with the disfigurement, Brahe fashioned a replacement nose out of a gold and silver alloy. His new nose was not only functional but also a symbol of his indomitable spirit.

An Unconventional Residence

Brahe's passion for astronomy led him to construct a state-of-the-art observatory on the island of Hven, in what is now Sweden. Known as Uraniborg (meaning "Castle of the Heavens"), this grand observatory featured custom-built instruments for tracking celestial bodies. It was an opulent and eccentric home for an astronomer, complete with luxurious furnishings, a pet elk, and even a dwarf jester.

The Unprecedented Precision

One of Brahe's most significant contributions to astronomy was his meticulous and highly precise observations of the night sky. Armed with his specially designed instruments, he cataloged the positions of stars and planets with unparalleled accuracy. Brahe's observations provided the raw data that Johannes Kepler would later use to formulate his laws of planetary motion, revolutionising our understanding of the solar system.

Despite the eccentricities of his life, Brahe's commitment to precision made him an invaluable figure in the history of astronomy.

The Great Comet Controversy

In 1577, a brilliant comet blazed across the night sky, captivating astronomers and laypeople alike. Brahe seized this opportunity to make a name for himself by publishing an astronomical treatise on the comet's appearance, documenting its position and trajectory.

His observations dispelled the prevailing belief that comets were atmospheric phenomena and instead demonstrated that they were celestial objects. This discovery challenged established ideas about the heavens and solidified Brahe's reputation as a leading astronomer of his time.

The Tychonic System

Brahe's work on the solar system culminated in the development of the Tychonic system, a hybrid model that attempted to reconcile the geocentric and heliocentric views of the universe. In this model, the Earth remained stationary at the centre of the cosmos, while the other planets orbited the Sun.

While Brahe's system eventually gave way to Kepler's more accurate heliocentric model, it represented a significant step in the transition from ancient geocentrism to modern understanding of planetary motion.

The Star-Crossed Collaboration

Tycho Brahe's career also involved a fruitful collaboration with Johannes Kepler, a brilliant mathematician and astronomer. Although their personalities clashed, with Brahe being known for his authoritarian demeanour and Kepler for his independent spirit, their partnership was crucial.

Kepler used Brahe's extensive data to develop his laws of planetary motion, proving that the planets orbited the Sun in ellipses rather than circles. This groundbreaking work revolutionised our understanding of celestial mechanics and laid the foundation for Isaac Newton's laws of gravitation.

The Mysterious End

Tycho Brahe's life came to a tragic and mysterious end in 1601. He fell ill and died after attending a banquet, but the exact cause of his death remains a subject of debate. Some speculate that he succumbed to mercury poisoning from his golden nose, while others suggest a urinary infection.

"Behold, directly overhead, a certain strange star was suddenly seen... amazed, and as if astonished and stupefied, I stood still."
- Tycho Brahe

Matthew Hopkins - The Witchfinder General

Known as the "Witchfinder General," Hopkins played a pivotal and notorious role in the persecution of alleged witches in England during a time of superstition, fear, and moral hysteria.

The Witch Hunts Unleashed

Matthew Hopkins was born in Great Wenham, Suffolk, England, in 1620. He came of age during a tumultuous period in England's history, marked by political instability, religious fervor, and social upheaval. It was against this backdrop that he embarked on a career that would make him infamous.

The Pendle Witch Trials

Hopkins first gained prominence as a witch-hunter during the Pendle witch trials of 1612. The trials, held in Lancashire, were among the most infamous witchcraft trials in English history. Accusations of witchcraft were widespread, and Hopkins's zeal for hunting witches led him to offer his services as an "expert" witchfinder.

During the trials, Hopkins used dubious methods to extract confessions from the accused, including sleep deprivation, physical torture, and "witch-pricking," in which suspects were examined for supposed witch's marks or "devil's teats." These methods, while horrifying, were tragically consistent with the prevailing beliefs of the time.

The Discovery of Witchcraft

In 1647, Hopkins published a book titled "The Discovery of Witchcraft," which outlined his views on witchcraft and his methods for identifying witches. Although he was not the author of this work (it was written by Reginald Scot in 1584), Hopkins used it to lend an air of legitimacy to his witch-hunting activities.

"The Discovery of Witchcraft" was critical of witch hunts and questioned the existence of witches. However, Hopkins used selected passages to justify his witch-hunting endeavours, reinforcing his own self-proclaimed expertise.

The Witchfinder General

It was in the early 1640s that Matthew Hopkins began his career as a professional witch-hunter. He assumed the title of "Witchfinder General" and traveled throughout East Anglia, offering his services to towns and villages plagued by witchcraft accusations.
Hopkins was not an official government appointee but rather a self-styled expert who profited from the prevailing fear of witchcraft. He charged fees for his services, which included the identification, examination, and trial of suspected witches. His methods were ruthless, and he often relied on coerced confessions and spectral evidence.

The Witch-Hunting Techniques

Hopkins employed a variety of techniques to identify and convict alleged witches. These methods included:
Witch Pricking: Using a long needle or pin, Hopkins and his associates would search the accused for "witch's marks" believed to be insensible to pain.

Dunking: Suspected witches were bound and thrown into bodies of water. If they floated, they were deemed witches; if they sank, they were considered innocent but often drowned.

Witch Tests: Hopkins employed various tests, such as having the accused recite the Lord's Prayer flawlessly. Failure to do so was seen as evidence of witchcraft.

Forced Confessions: Hopkins and his assistants subjected suspects to sleep deprivation and physical torture until they confessed to being witches.

These methods, while cruel and unscientific, were widely accepted in an era of superstition and moral panic. Hopkins's reputation as an expert in identifying witches fueled the hysteria and fear surrounding witchcraft.

The Toll of the Witch Hunts

Matthew Hopkins's witch hunts had devastating consequences. Scores of individuals, primarily women, were accused, tried, and executed as witches based on flimsy evidence and coerced confessions. The exact number of victims is difficult to ascertain, but estimates suggest that hundreds may have perished due to witch hunts in East Anglia during his tenure as Witchfinder General.

The trials and executions wreaked havoc on communities, tearing apart families and sowing mistrust among neighbours. The witch hunts left a lasting legacy of fear and paranoia, with the spectre of witchcraft continuing to haunt the collective imagination for centuries.

The Decline of the Witchfinder General

Matthew Hopkins's career as Witchfinder General was relatively short-lived. His methods and actions began to draw criticism and skepticism, even in a society gripped by witch hysteria. Some authorities questioned the validity of his methods, and he faced increasing resistance from those who believed his witch hunts were unjust.

In 1647, Hopkins and his associate John Stearne published "The Discovery of Witches," a manual that outlined their methods and experiences as witch-hunters. While the book reinforced their own beliefs, it did little to convince the growing number of skeptics.

Legacy and Impact

Matthew Hopkins died in 1647 at the age of 27. His death marked the end of his reign as Witchfinder General, but the legacy of his witch hunts endured. The fear and paranoia surrounding witchcraft persisted for years, leading to additional witch trials and executions across England and the American colonies.

In the centuries that followed, society came to view the witch hunts as a dark chapter in history, driven by ignorance and superstition. Hopkins's methods, once seen as legitimate, became symbols of injustice and cruelty.

Matthew Hopkins, the Witchfinder General, played a significant role in the witch hunts of the 17th century. His methods, fuelled by superstition and fear, led to the persecution and execution of many innocent individuals accused of witchcraft. Hopkins's legacy is a stark reminder of the dangers of moral hysteria and the devastating consequences of witch hunts.

While the witch hunts of the past may seem distant, their echoes continue to resonate in the ongoing struggle for justice and the importance of critical thinking in the face of fear and prejudice.

Treasures Untold - Legendary Pirates of the Golden Age

Today, the word 'pirate' immediately conjures images of swashbuckling rogues, with wry smiles and razor-sharp wits. However, there was once a time where such a word wrought sheer terror. In an age of sail, pirates represented the ultimate threat to civilisation and progress, but that doesn't mean they were uncivilised themselves; they most certainly made the most of their ill begotten goods.

Blackbeard - The Legend of Terror on the High Seas

The Beginnings of a Maritime Menace

Edward Teach was born around 1680 in Bristol, England, and little is known about his early life. He likely had a naval background, as his experience with ships and navigation became evident during his piratical career.

Teach's transformation into Blackbeard began when he joined the crew of the pirate Benjamin Hornigold in the early 18th century. Under Hornigold's tutelage, Teach honed his skills as a pirate and gained a reputation for both audacity and ruthlessness.

It was during this time that Teach adopted his now-infamous persona—Blackbeard. He grew a thick black beard that he tied with slow-burning fuses and lit during battles. The sight of his face shrouded in smoke and framed by his burning beard was a terrifying spectacle that struck fear into the hearts of his enemies.

Blackbeard's career as a pirate was marked by audacious attacks, clever tactics, and a fearsome image. He often used intimidation to secure the surrender of his targets without a fight, relying on his fearsome appearance and reputation.

The Queen Anne's Revenge

One of Blackbeard's most famous actions was the capture of a French slave ship, La Concorde, which he renamed the Queen Anne's Revenge. The ship was a massive warship, heavily armed and capable of striking fear into anyone who saw it on the horizon.
With the Queen Anne's Revenge as his flagship, Blackbeard launched a series of successful raids and attacks along the American coast, particularly in the Caribbean and the eastern seaboard.

Dancing the Charleston

One of Blackbeard's most audacious acts was the blockade of Charleston, South Carolina, in May 1718. With a fleet of ships under his command, including the Queen Anne's Revenge, Blackbeard effectively cut off the city's access to maritime trade. The blockade created panic and economic disruption in Charleston, forcing the colonial government to offer a hefty ransom in exchange for the city's release from Blackbeard's grasp.

A Captain Goes Down With His Ship

Blackbeard's reign of terror eventually drew the attention of colonial authorities and the Royal Navy. In November 1718, Lieutenant Robert Maynard of the Royal Navy was dispatched to confront Blackbeard.
The two forces clashed in a ferocious battle off the coast of North Carolina, near Ocracoke Island. Despite being outnumbered and outgunned, Blackbeard and his crew fought fiercely. The battle was brutal, with hand-to-hand combat on the decks of the ships.
In the end, Blackbeard was mortally wounded, sustaining multiple gunshot wounds and deep cuts. He fought on until he was overwhelmed, eventually succumbing to his injuries.
Legend has it that he was decapitated, and his severed head was

hung from the bowsprit of Maynard's ship as a gruesome trophy.

Blackbeard's legacy as a pirate has left an indelible mark on pirate lore and popular culture. His fearsome image, ruthless tactics, and audacious raids have inspired countless tales of piracy, both in fiction and history.

Stede Bonnet - The Gentleman Pirate

A Silver Spoon

Born into a wealthy English family on the island of Barbados in 1688, Stede Bonnet was far from the image of the destitute and desperate pirate often portrayed in legends. His father, Edward Bonnet, was a prosperous landowner and plantation owner. Bonnet himself led a comfortable life as a landowner, husband, and father, earning him the nickname "The Gentleman of Barbados."

So, what drove a man of privilege to forsake his comfortable life and embark on a perilous journey into piracy? The answer to this question lies in Bonnet's personality and a series of unexpected events.

High Society to High Seas

Bonnet's early life was marked by an adventurous spirit that deviated from the expectations of a typical gentleman. He was well-educated and could read and write, but he possessed a restlessness that led him to the sea. In his mid-thirties, Bonnet decided to leave behind his family, plantation, and the genteel life in Barbados to become a pirate.

His motivations for this radical departure remain a subject of debate among historians. Some speculate that he may have been suffering from what we now recognise as a mid-life crisis, while others suggest he was seeking excitement and adventure to escape the monotony of his privileged life.

With no prior experience in seafaring or piracy, Bonnet purchased a ship, a French-built sloop which he renamed the "Revenge." He then embarked on a crash course in piracy, assembling a crew of hardened buccaneers who would serve as his mentors. His lack of maritime knowledge, however, earned him the derisive nickname "Captain Every."

The Revenge was armed with ten cannons and a crew of approximately seventy men. Bonnet, now calling himself

"Captain Thomas," was ready to set sail on a new and unexpected chapter in his life.

Short but Sweet Career

Bonnet's piracy career, which lasted less than two years, was marked by a series of audacious and, at times, baffling exploits. His actions defied the traditional image of pirates who often emerged from impoverished backgrounds and sought riches and revenge against oppressive authorities.

In September 1717, Bonnet led the Revenge to the coast of South Carolina, where he orchestrated one of his most bombastic attacks—assaulting the heavily defended Charleston Harbour. His decision to attack one of the most fortified ports in the American colonies was both audacious and reckless. The attack, while not ultimately successful, was a bold move that showcased Bonnet's determination and his crew's loyalty. The audacity of a landowner-turned-pirate attacking a major colonial city left many baffled and intrigued.

Taming the Terror

In another surprising turn of events, Bonnet formed an alliance with the infamous Blackbeard (Edward Teach). Blackbeard's reputation as one of the fiercest and most ruthless pirates of the era contrasted starkly with Bonnet's background as a gentleman. The two captains joined forces for a time, engaging in piracy along the eastern seaboard of North America.

Their partnership, however, was short-lived, as Blackbeard eventually betrayed Bonnet, leaving him and some of his crew stranded on an isolated island. This episode highlighted Bonnet's vulnerability in the cutthroat world of piracy, where alliances were often tenuous and self-preservation was paramount.

A Dignified End

Bonnet's luck eventually ran out when he was captured in 1718 by the British Navy off the coast of North Carolina. His capture led to a trial, during which he tried to invoke a pardon for his previous acts of piracy. His plea was unsuccessful, and he was sentenced to hang.

During his imprisonment, Bonnet's gentlemanly demeanour and insistence on being addressed as "Captain" endeared him to some of the local authorities. There were even appeals for clemency on his behalf, arguing that he had been led into piracy by bad influences and deserved mercy.

On December 10, 1718, Stede Bonnet met his end on the gallows in Charleston, South Carolina. His execution marked the final chapter of a remarkable and perplexing life that had taken him from the comfort of Barbados to the treacherous world of piracy.

Bonnet's legacy is one of contradictions. He was a wealthy landowner who abandoned his privileged life for a perilous existence at sea. He was a gentleman who sought adventure as a pirate, earning the respect of some and the scorn of others. His audacious attack on Charleston Harbour and his ill-fated alliance with Blackbeard remain memorable chapters in the annals of piracy.

Bartholomew Roberts - The Pirate King

A Paupers Birth

Born in 1682 in Pembrokeshire, Wales, Bartholomew Roberts had a rather unassuming beginning for someone who would go on to become one of history's most notorious pirates. Little is known about his early life and family, but it is believed that he came from a humble background.

Roberts's life took an unexpected turn in 1719 when he found himself aboard the slave ship Princess, which was captured by pirate Captain Howell Davis off the coast of West Africa. Roberts and the other crew members were forced into piracy or joined willingly, setting the stage for his transformation from an ordinary sailor to a feared pirate captain.

The Prince of the Princess

Roberts's ascent in the pirate hierarchy was swift and dramatic. After Howell Davis was killed in a confrontation with Portuguese forces, Roberts was elected as the new captain by the crew. This election marked the beginning of his illustrious and audacious career as a pirate leader.

One of the defining aspects of Roberts's leadership was his implementation of a "pirate code." This code outlined rules and regulations for the crew, emphasising fairness, democracy, and discipline. Roberts believed in treating his crew well, and he forbade drunkenness and gambling on board, unlike many other pirate crews of the time.

The pirate code also included provisions for dividing plunder, ensuring that the crew received a fair share of the spoils. Roberts's leadership style and adherence to a code of conduct helped foster loyalty and unity among his crew.

A Reign of Fear

Under Roberts's command, his pirate crew became a formidable force on the high seas. They attacked and plundered numerous ships, earning a reputation for their audacity and ferocity. Roberts was known for employing clever tactics, such as disguising his ship as a merchant vessel to get close to unsuspecting targets.

One of his most famous captures was the Royal Fortune, a former French slave ship that he outfitted with 42 cannons, making it a formidable warship. With this powerful vessel at his disposal, Roberts went on to raid and capture numerous ships, including those belonging to the powerful British Royal Navy.

The Pirate King

Perhaps the most remarkable achievement of Roberts's career was his self-proclamation as the "Pirate King." In a time when piracy was marked by fierce competition and rivalries among pirate captains, Roberts managed to earn the respect and allegiance of many other pirates.

Roberts's audacious and successful attacks on British and Portuguese vessels in the Atlantic and Caribbean waters contributed to his reputation as a pirate king. His ability to unite pirates from different crews under his command was a testament to his leadership skills and charisma.

Divine Wrath

Despite his formidable successes, Bartholomew Roberts's life as a pirate captain was destined to be short-lived. In February 1722, while anchored off the coast of Africa, his ship, the Royal Fortune, fell prey to a sudden and devastating storm. The ship was severely damaged, and Roberts himself was killed by a direct hit from a cannonball.

The death of Roberts marked the end of an era in piracy. His reign as the "Pirate King" was over, but his legacy endured in adventures of his crew.

The Grave Robbers' Grand Caper - Burke, Hare, and the Body Snatching Shenanigans of the 19th Century

In the colourful tapestry of the 19th century, where top hats and corsets reigned supreme, a curious underworld of body snatchers and grave robbers thrived. Among them, the infamous duo Burke and Hare emerged as the Bonnie and Clyde of the body-snatching world. But they were far from the only ones in this macabre trade.

The Resurrection Men Rise

The 19th century witnessed a surge in the demand for cadavers, driven by the blossoming field of medical education and research. As medical schools clamoured for bodies to dissect, a peculiar profession emerged – the resurrection man, colloquially known as a grave robber.

Resurrection men were enterprising individuals who made it their mission to procure freshly buried bodies for the medical profession. They operated on the fringes of society, often under the cloak of darkness and with a penchant for mischief.

Enter William Burke and William Hare, two Irishmen who elevated grave robbing to a nefarious art form. Their story reads like a dark comedy of errors with a macabre twist.

Burke and Hare hailed from Edinburgh, Scotland, where they stumbled upon an ingenious business opportunity. Instead of waiting for someone to die, they decided to expedite the process by turning to murder. It was a rather morbid form of efficiency.

Over a span of several months, the duo embarked on a murderous spree, luring unsuspecting victims to their deaths. Their modus operandi was as absurd as it was sinister. They suffocated their victims, often with a hand over the mouth and a pillow over the face, to ensure a quick and quiet demise.

A Lesson in Anatomy

After dispatching their victims, Burke and Hare delivered the bodies to a local anatomist, Dr. Robert Knox, who paid handsomely for the fresh specimens. It was an unscrupulous partnership that had grave consequences.
As their activities escalated, Burke and Hare became embroiled in a series of darkly comic misadventures. In one instance, a botched attempt to suffocate a victim led to a sudden and rather inconvenient bout of snoring. They narrowly escaped detection by convincing Dr. Knox that their victim was merely in a deep slumber.
In another comical twist, one of their victims, a well-known local beggar named Joseph, proved rather problematic in death. His distinctive appearance became a source of concern, as his body risked recognition. To remedy the situation, Dr. Knox commissioned a death mask, ensuring the beggar's notoriety lived on in a macabre fashion.

The Dark Laughter Ends

Burke and Hare's reign of terror came to a halt when an anatomical lecturer grew suspicious of their frequent deliveries. He alerted the authorities, leading to the discovery of multiple bodies hidden within Burke and Hare's lodgings.
The ensuing trial, with its blend of horror and absurdity, captivated the public. Burke was ultimately found guilty of murder and sentenced to hang. Hare, on the other hand, escaped with his life in exchange for his damning testimony.
While Burke paid the ultimate price for his deeds, the legacy of his and Hare's dark exploits endures. Their story serves as a cautionary tale of the bizarre and treacherous world of 19th-century grave robbing.

A Grave Affair

In the annals of history, Burke and Hare stand as a peculiar pair, whose dark deeds danced on the fringes of a world where comedy and tragedy intermingle. Their story reminds us that even the most morbid of chapters can be tinged with a peculiar, dark humour.

So, the next time you find yourself perusing a medical textbook or strolling through an old cemetery, spare a thought for the body snatchers and grave robbers who once revelled in their mischievous pursuits. After all, they added a dash of dark hilarity to a world that desperately needed it.

"Murder is always a mistake. One should never do anything that one cannot talk about after dinner."
- *Oscar Wilde*

High Stakes Action - The Real-Life Vampires of History

In the 21st century, when we picture a 'vampire', an imagine may spring to mind of a deviously alluring, yet dangerous, individual. The charm and beauty often associated with these bloodsucking fiends today is a relatively modern invention. Whilst beauty has almost always been an inherent aspect of vampiric beings, we are all too eager to forget that it belies a much darker truth; vampires are, by nature, reflective of the innate human fallibility for greed, lust, and pride.

Vlad Tepes: The Impaler Extraordinaire

Once upon a time, in the dark and brooding land of Transylvania, there lived a man whose name would send shivers down the spine of history: Vlad Tepes, also known as Vlad the Impaler. This guy didn't just walk on the dark side; he practically built a summer home there. With a reputation so ruthless it could give nightmares to Freddy Krueger, Vlad Tepes stands as a macabre icon of cruelty and creative problem-solving.

Pride and Prejudice and Torture

Vlad Tepes wasn't always a master of impalement. In his youth, he was held hostage by the Ottoman Empire. This little "vacation" allowed him to witness firsthand the Ottomans' penchant for sticking people on spikes. Little did they know, they were schooling the Impaler-to-be.

Upon reclaiming his throne, Vlad decided that regular old execution methods just didn't cut it. So, he went for the shock factor. Impalement, a method of sticking people on tall, pointy stakes, became his signature move. It was like he watched a vampire flick and thought, "Hold my blood goblet."

The Art of Sticking It to 'Em

Vlad's impalement extravaganza wasn't a one-time deal. No, he went for quantity over quality. He impaled thousands of people, from criminals to political rivals. His motto? "If you can't beat 'em, skewer 'em!"

One of Vlad's greatest hits was the "Forest of the Impaled." Imagine a sinister garden with human popsicles as the décor. It was his way of saying, "Welcome to my twisted wonderland."

Vlad loved to throw parties, but his soirées were more "shock and awe" than champagne and canapés. He'd invite guests, and surprise! They'd find themselves impaled right there at the dinner table. Talk about a killer host.

Impaler Strikes Back

Vlad wasn't content with just impaling folks; he also took on the mighty Ottoman Empire. He'd impale Ottoman soldiers and send the survivors back to their sultan with a message: "Not today, pal."

Eventually, Vlad's impalement spree caught up with him. The Ottomans defeated him, and he had to flee. But don't worry, he left plenty of impaled memories behind.

Legacy of the Impaler

Vlad's ruthless reputation inspired Bram Stoker's iconic vampire, Dracula. But let's be clear, Dracula had more flair for seduction than Vlad. Bram Stoker took the impaler, gave him fangs, and the rest is cinematic history.

Vlad Tepes left an indelible mark on history. His creative use of impalement is a masterclass in sadistic innovation. While his methods were brutal, there's no denying that he's earned his place in the annals of history as the Impaler Extraordinaire.

So, if you ever find yourself in Transylvania and hear the rustling of leaves in the dark, just remember, it might not be a vampire–it could be the ghost of Vlad Tepes, still impaling hearts with his macabre legend.

Elizabeth Bathory: The Blood Countess Who Took "Beauty Sleep" to a Whole New Level

1560, in the chilling heart of Hungary, there lived a woman whose beauty regime would make even the most dedicated skincare influencer shudder. Her name was Elizabeth Bathory, but she's more famously known as the Blood Countess. If Vlad the Impaler had a distant, equally macabre cousin, it would be her. Let's take a deep dive into the sinister world of this beauty-obsessed noblewoman.

Blood is the New Botox

Elizabeth Bathory was born into Hungarian nobility in the late 16th century. With her privileged upbringing, she had all the time in the world to ponder life's big questions, like, "How can I stay young forever?"

Elizabeth was obsessed with the idea of preserving her youthful beauty. So obsessed, in fact, that she believed bathing in the blood of virgins would do the trick. Talk about taking "beauty sleep" to a whole new level!

The Accusations Begin

Rumours of Elizabeth's ghastly beauty regimen soon spread like wildfire. It was alleged that she and her loyal servants embarked on a spree of abductions, torture, and bloodletting that would make Dracula blush.

Elizabeth's castle became ground zero for her dark experiments. It was said to be filled with secret chambers and torture devices, which she used to extract the precious life essence of her victims.

The Trial of the Blood Countess

Elizabeth's reign of alleged terror eventually caught up with her. Her servants were arrested and put on trial, revealing horrifying details of their lady's gruesome beauty rituals. The trial was like a real-life episode of a vampire-themed courtroom drama. The truth about Elizabeth Bathory's crimes remains a subject of historical debate. Some believe she was unfairly targeted for her wealth and influence, while others see her as a sadistic killer. It's like a historical whodunit that even Sherlock Holmes would find perplexing.

Bathing in the Blood of Pop Culture

Elizabeth Bathory's tale has left an indelible mark on pop culture. From horror movies to metal band lyrics, her story continues to inspire the darkest corners of artistic expression. What is it about Elizabeth Bathory that continues to captivate our imaginations? Is it her obsession with youth, her gruesome beauty rituals, or simply the irresistible allure of a female villain who defies gender norms? Whatever it is, she's here to stay. Elizabeth Bathory, the Blood Countess, remains an enigmatic figure in history. Whether she was a misunderstood beauty enthusiast or a ruthless killer, her legacy endures as a testament to the intersection of vanity, violence, and the eternal quest for youth.

Jure Grando - The Terror of Istria

The tale of Jure Grando unfolded in the picturesque region of Istria, a peninsula located in modern-day Croatia. Istria, with its charming villages, fertile plains, and rugged coastline along the Adriatic Sea, was home to a close-knit community of farmers and villagers in the early 18th century. It was against this rustic backdrop that the legend of Jure Grando took root and grew to become one of the earliest recorded vampire accounts in Europe.

Death is only the Beginning

The story of Jure Grando began with his death in 1656. At this time, vampire folklore and superstitions about the undead were pervasive throughout Europe. These beliefs often revolved around the fear of individuals returning from the dead to prey upon the living. Jure Grando's legend emerged from a combination of local superstitions, fear, and unexplained events.

A Late-Night Visitor

The chain of events that would culminate in the legend of Jure Grando began with the passing of Jure Grando himself. In death, he became the central figure of a chilling narrative. It was said that shortly after his burial, Grando's corpse rose from the grave.

The villagers of Kringa, where Grando had lived, soon began to experience a series of disturbing nocturnal visits. Those who claimed to have encountered Grando reported that he would appear at their doorsteps during the dark hours of the night, knocking insistently. He would beg for food, request to be let inside their homes, or simply stand menacingly on their doorsteps.

The descriptions of Grando during these visits were consistent and unsettling. He appeared pale, with hollow eyes that seemed to burn with malevolent intent. His attire, though burial clothes, was said to be in pristine condition, as though he had never been interred.

Grando's nighttime appearances continued to escalate in frequency and audacity, plunging the once-peaceful village of Kringa into a state of unrelenting fear. The villagers believed they were being tormented by a creature known as a "nosferatu" or vampire. This term was used in the Istrian region to describe a vampire-like being that rose from the grave to prey upon the living.

The Uprising

As terror gripped Kringa, the villagers felt compelled to take action against the nocturnal menace. The local priest, Father Giorgio, emerged as a central figure in this unfolding drama. With a group of brave individuals from the community, he embarked on a mission to confront the alleged vampire.

Father Giorgio and his group confronted Jure Grando at his gravesite during one of his nocturnal visits. Armed with holy symbols, crosses, and a profound determination, they demanded that Grando return to his eternal rest and cease his menacing activities.

Initially, Grando resisted the efforts to subdue him. He vehemently rejected the exorcisms and commands issued by Father Giorgio. The confrontation was described as intense, with Grando displaying an unnatural strength and resolve.

Despite the vampire's resistance, the collective efforts of the group gradually began to wear him down. The persistence of Father Giorgio, his prayers, and the power of the religious symbols began to take their toll on Grando.

Under the relentless pressure, Grando finally relented. It is said that he acknowledged the authority of the priest and acquiesced to the demands. With that, he retreated to his grave, never to trouble the living of Kringa again.

Laid to Rest

Jure Grando, once a source of terror and dread, was laid to rest once more, but this time with a massive stone placed upon his burial site. It was believed that this final act would ensure that he remained in his grave for eternity, bringing an end to the vampire's nocturnal visits and restoring peace to the village of Kringa.

Sir Hiram Maxim - The Machine Maverick

In the annals of invention and engineering, there are those who chart a steady course, and then there are those who soar to heights of creativity that defy convention. Sir Hiram Maxim was undoubtedly one of the latter—a man whose name became synonymous with innovation and engineering prowess.

A Life Set for Flight

Hiram Maxim was born on February 5, 1840, in Sangerville, Maine, USA. From a young age, he displayed a remarkable curiosity about the world around him, particularly in the fields of engineering and invention. This innate curiosity would drive him to pursue pioneering feats in aviation and weaponry. In 1881, Maxim relocated to the United Kingdom, lured by the promise of opportunities in Europe's burgeoning industrial landscape. It was in the UK that he would establish himself as a prolific inventor, etching his name into the annals of engineering history.

Revolutionising Warfare

Maxim's first claim to fame came with the invention of the Maxim Gun, the world's first portable, fully automatic machine gun. This firearm was nothing short of a game-changer in military history, drastically altering the dynamics of armed conflict. The key innovation behind the Maxim Gun was its use of recoil energy to automatically cycle the firing mechanism. This allowed for a rapid and sustained rate of fire—up to 600 rounds per minute. The Maxim Gun became the standard machine gun for many militaries around the world and played a significant role in late 19th and early 20th-century conflicts.

Dreams of Soaring Skies

While Maxim's fame as the inventor of the machine gun was firmly established, his passion for aviation was equally fervent. In the late 19th century, the possibility of powered flight was a tantalising dream shared by many inventors. Maxim was determined to turn that dream into reality.

Maxim's pursuit of flight led to the creation of the Captive Flying Machine, a colossal contraption that resembled a cross between a carousel and a roller coaster. It consisted of a circular track with a central tower, from which a flying machine—attached to a cable—could be propelled along the track.

The Captive Flying Machine allowed people to experience simulated flight. It was not a true flying machine in the sense of achieving sustained, controlled flight, but rather a precursor to amusement park rides that would follow in its wake. Visitors to Maxim's amusement park, located at his estate in Kent, could experience the sensation of soaring through the air.

A Vision Takes Flight

Maxim's vision for flight extended beyond amusement park rides. He envisioned the creation of a true flying machine, and in 1894, he unveiled his concept for the "Battleplane." This was a revolutionary idea that combined elements of both aircraft and armoured vehicles.

The Battleplane concept featured a large, winged machine with a central fuselage designed to carry soldiers and weapons. It was intended to be both a flying fortress and a means of transport for military personnel. While the Battleplane never took flight, it was an early exploration of the potential applications of aviation in warfare.

Flying High with the Maxim-Bleriot Airship

Maxim's foray into aviation continued with his involvement in the Maxim-Bleriot Airship, a partnership with French aviation pioneer Louis Bleriot. This project aimed to create a navigable airship capable of carrying passengers and cargo.

The Maxim-Bleriot Airship featured a unique design with a central gondola suspended beneath a cylindrical gas bag. It was a departure from traditional rigid airships and offered improved stability and manoeuvrability. While the project faced challenges and never achieved commercial success, it showcased Maxim's willingness to explore innovative concepts in aviation.

The End of an Era

Sir Hiram Maxim passed away on November 24, 1916, leaving behind a legacy that bridged the worlds of firearms, aviation, and engineering. His contributions to military technology had a profound impact on the course of history, and his imaginative explorations in aviation laid the groundwork for future developments in flight.

A Cereal Offender - The Cruel Oddities of John Harvey Kellogg

John Harvey Kellogg, yes, the very same Kellogg who started the globally famous cereal brand, was a controversial figure in the early development of public health movements. An associate of the Seventh Day Adventist church and advocate for a range of bizarre and dangerous practices, it's safe to say his legacy is as controversial as it is fascinating. Among his many strange contributions to society are:

Vegetarianism and Health Reform: Kellogg was a staunch advocate of vegetarianism and believed that a plant-based diet was essential for good health. He promoted this diet at his Battle Creek Sanitarium and in his writings.

Anti-Masturbation Crusade: One of Kellogg's most peculiar beliefs was his strong opposition to masturbation, which he considered a dangerous and sinful practice. He advocated for various measures to prevent it, including circumcision and the use of carbolic acid on young boys' genitalia. As much as 80% of the male population of the US is circumcised (as of 2019) as a direct result of Kellogg's crusade.

Kellogg's Cornflakes: While Kellogg's invention of cornflakes revolutionised the breakfast cereal industry, he originally created them as part of his belief in a bland, vegetarian diet that would discourage indulgence in rich or stimulating foods. He believed that the bland flavour of the previously unsweetened cereal would be so soul-crushingly boring that it would deter from any degree of sexual desire. He was wrong.

Colon Health Obsession: Kellogg had an obsession with colon health and advocated for regular enemas, often administering them to patients at his sanitarium. He believed that a clean colon was essential for overall well-being; even going so far as to experiment with the use of yoghurt enemas. Fortunately this practice didn't catch on, I can only imagine why.

Eugenics and Controversial Views: Kellogg held eugenic views and believed in selective breeding to improve the human race. He advocated for the sterilisation of individuals with certain conditions, which is now widely regarded as a controversial and unethical stance. He keenly supported the pseudoscience of phrenology, wherein practitioners measured skull dimensions and morphology to predict criminal or 'unholy' behaviours. The practice was frequently used to enforce racist and ableist practices, such as the sterilisation of ethnic minorities.

Family Feud: Kellogg had a bitter and long-lasting feud with his brother, Will Keith Kellogg, over the commercialisation of cornflakes. While John Harvey Kellogg wanted to maintain strict control over the cereal's production, Will saw its commercial potential and founded the Kellogg Company, leading to their estrangement. Fortunately, Will also added sugar to the recipe, resulting in the creation of todays most popular breakfast foodstuffs.

Influence on Wellness Movements: Despite his eccentric, and often cruel, beliefs, Kellogg's influence on health and wellness movements is undeniable. His promotion of a plant-based diet, exercise, and the importance of whole grains contributed to the development of many modern wellness practices.

The Dane Hills Horror - Black Annis

Deep within the folklore of Leicestershire, England, lurks the ominous presence of Black Annis, a fearsome and legendary hag who has haunted the collective imagination for centuries. Her dark and terrifying tale weaves a chilling thread through the tapestry of English folklore.

Ghastly Origins

The legend of Black Annis is most closely associated with the English county of Leicestershire, particularly the rural areas around the town of Leicester. Her name has been linked to the local dialect, with "Annis" believed to be a variation of "Agnes" or "Ann," and "Black" denoting her sinister nature.

Black Annis is described as a hideous hag with blue skin, a monstrous mouth filled with sharp teeth, and long, claw-like fingers. She is often depicted wearing a tattered, black cloak made from the skins of her victims. The grim appearance of Black Annis has fueled fear and fascination for generations.

One of the most prominent aspects of Black Annis's legend is her lair in the Dane Hills near Leicester. There, she is said to reside in a cave or hollowed-out tree, emerging under the cover of darkness to hunt for unwary travelers or, more ominously, children who have misbehaved.

Black Annis's sinister reputation stems from her gruesome appetite for human flesh, particularly the flesh of children. At night, she is said to descend from the hill and lurk outside the windows of houses, listening for the sound of crying children. Her long talons sometimes tap at the windows, where they often go unnoticed by adults, due to their resemblance to tree branches; there she lures the young into her icy grasp. With her quarry in her clutches, the cobalt hag flees, carrying them away to her lair to be devoured. Her macabre taste is the stuff of nightmares.

Making Sense of Evil

The legend of Black Annis has played a role in local traditions, with stories of her used to scare children into good behavior. Folk remedies and amulets were also employed to ward off her malevolent presence, such as hanging a rowan tree branch or iron horseshoe above doorways for protection.

Black Annis is a dark embodiment of the primal fears that have haunted humanity for generations. She serves as a cautionary figure, a symbol of the unknown terrors that await in the darkness. Her legend has become an enduring part of English folklore, a reminder of the power of storytelling to evoke both dread and fascination.

'Behold A Man!' - The Musings of Diogenes

Diogenes of Sinope, a Greek philosopher born around 412 or 404 BCE, remains one of the most eccentric and memorable figures in the history of philosophy. As the founder of the Cynic school, he lived a life marked by deliberate simplicity, unconventional behaviour, and a sharp wit that challenged societal norms and the values of his time.

The Cynic Philosophy

Diogenes was a staunch adherent of Cynicism, a philosophical school that emphasised living in accordance with nature and rejecting societal conventions. Cynics believed that true happiness and virtue could be found through a minimalist and ascetic lifestyle.

Diogenes famously eschewed material possessions and luxuries. He was known for his rejection of the traditional Greek lifestyle, choosing instead to live homeless and destitute. He would often sleep in a large ceramic jar (or "pithos") and wander the streets barefoot.

One of Diogenes's most famous acts was his search for an honest man. He would walk through the streets of Athens in broad daylight with a lantern, claiming to be searching for an honest person but never finding one. This act was a satirical commentary on the perceived moral decay of Athenian society.

Philosophical Parables

Diogenes was notorious for his bluntness and irreverence. When asked what wine he liked best, he replied, "That which belongs to another." He once urinated on a bystander who criticised him, saying, "If only it were as easy to banish hunger by rubbing one's belly."

Diogenes often used parables and anecdotes to convey his philosophical ideas. For instance, when criticised for drinking wine, he replied by pouring out his cup and saying, "What I like best is wine, and when it has not been mixed with water."

This illustrated his belief in the importance of authenticity and simplicity.
Diogenes used his unconventional behaviour to make pointed social and political statements. He believed that societal norms and conventions were often empty and hypocritical. By living in a manner that defied these norms, he aimed to expose their shallowness.

A Profound Legacy
Diogenes's legacy endures through the writings of his contemporaries, including the philosopher Plato, who was both impressed and bemused by him. The term "cynic" itself derives from the Greek word "kynikos," meaning "dog-like," possibly because of Diogenes's simple and unrefined lifestyle.

"Even if I am but a pretender to wisdom, that in itself is a philosophy!"
- Diogenes of Sinope

Chapter Four

Forbidden Science

Agent Orange - The Controversial Legacy

Developed during the Vietnam War era, this herbicide and defoliant was intended for use in military operations but would become infamous for its severe environmental and health consequences.

Origins of the Herbicide Program

The story of Agent Orange begins during the early stages of the Vietnam War when the United States sought ways to gain an advantage over the Viet Cong and North Vietnamese forces. The dense jungles and forests of Vietnam provided ample cover and made conventional military operations challenging. In response, the U.S. military explored the use of herbicides to defoliate the landscape, thus exposing the enemy's positions.

The Birth of Agent Orange

The development of Agent Orange was part of a broader program called Operation Ranch Hand. The U.S. military contracted with chemical companies to create herbicides, and in the process, a variety of chemical compounds were produced, each designated with a colour-coded stripe on its barrel. Agent Orange, named for the orange stripe, was one of the herbicides developed.

Agent Orange was a mixture of two herbicides, 2,4,5-T and 2,4-D, both of which were widely used in agriculture in the United States. While these compounds had been considered safe for crop management, they had not been tested for their long-term effects when sprayed on a massive scale in a tropical environment.

Military Deployment

From 1962 to 1971, Agent Orange and other herbicides were sprayed extensively across South Vietnam. The U.S. military conducted Operation Ranch Hand missions that involved aerial spraying of these herbicides over vast areas of jungle and

farmland. The goal was to destroy the dense vegetation that provided cover for the enemy, making it easier to detect and engage them.
The use of Agent Orange was not limited to military bases or combat zones. It was also used in areas where civilians lived and worked, leading to unintentional exposure among the local population.

Environmental and Health Consequences
The widespread use of Agent Orange had immediate and devastating environmental consequences. The herbicide stripped the jungles of their lush vegetation, turning once-thriving ecosystems into barren landscapes. It disrupted the delicate balance of these environments, causing long-lasting ecological damage.
However, the most tragic consequences of Agent Orange exposure were the health effects on both American veterans and Vietnamese civilians. The herbicide was contaminated with a highly toxic compound called dioxin, specifically 2,3,7,8-tetrachlorodibenzo-p-dioxin (TCDD). Dioxin is one of the most toxic substances known to science.

The Toll on Veterans
Many American military personnel who handled or were exposed to Agent Orange during their service in Vietnam experienced a range of health issues. These included various forms of cancer, respiratory problems, skin disorders, and birth defects in their offspring. The U.S. Department of Veterans Affairs recognised these health issues and established a program to provide medical care and compensation to affected veterans.
The recognition of Agent Orange-related illnesses among veterans sparked a decades-long debate about the responsibility of the U.S. government and the chemical companies involved in its production for the harm caused.

Impact on Vietnamese Civilians

The consequences of Agent Orange extended far beyond American veterans. Vietnamese civilians, particularly those living in the sprayed areas, faced severe health challenges. Rates of cancer, birth defects, and other illnesses surged in these regions. Many children born to parents who had been exposed to Agent Orange suffered from physical and cognitive disabilities.

The lasting health impact on the Vietnamese population remains a contentious issue, with differing opinions on the extent of the harm caused by Agent Orange. However, there is no doubt that the effects have been profound and tragic for many Vietnamese families.

Legal Battles and Compensation

In the years following the Vietnam War, veterans and their families, as well as affected Vietnamese citizens, pursued legal action against the U.S. government and the chemical companies involved in the production of Agent Orange. These legal battles aimed to secure compensation for the health problems caused by exposure to the herbicide.

In 1984, a landmark settlement was reached in a class-action lawsuit filed by U.S. veterans. The settlement established a fund of $180 million to provide compensation to veterans with illnesses related to Agent Orange exposure. Subsequent legal actions and settlements extended compensation to additional groups of affected individuals.

Environmental Remediation

The environmental damage caused by Agent Orange also led to efforts to remediate the affected areas. The U.S. government, in collaboration with the Vietnamese government and international organisations, initiated cleanup and reforestation projects in some of the most heavily sprayed regions. These efforts aimed to restore ecosystems and mitigate the long-term ecological impact of Agent Orange.

Agent Orange is a tragic chapter in both military history and environmental science. Its development and use, though initially intended to serve strategic military purposes, had far-reaching and devastating consequences for the environment and human health. The legacy of Agent Orange serves as a stark reminder of the ethical and humanitarian challenges posed by the use of toxic substances in warfare.

"It won't hurt you. It's just to kill plants. It's called Agent Orange... and it won't bother humans."
- *Karl Marlantes*

Lindow Man vs. Tollund Man - Dead Men Do Tell Tales

In the realm of archaeological discoveries, few are as captivating and enigmatic as the bog bodies - ancient human remains preserved in the depths of peat bogs. Among these preserved relics of the past, two figures stand out: the Lindow Man from Cheshire, England, and the Tollund Man from Denmark. These two individuals, separated by time and distance, share remarkable similarities in their fate, preservation, and the mysteries surrounding their lives and deaths.

The Lindow Man: England's John Doe

The Lindow Man, also known as Lindow II, emerged from the peat bog at Lindow Moss, Cheshire, England, in August 1984. Radiocarbon dating places him in the early Roman period, around 2 CE. His preservation, despite over 2,000 years in the bog, is nothing short of miraculous.

The unique conditions of the peat bog allowed the Lindow Man to survive with remarkable detail. His skin, hair, and even the stubble on his chin were preserved, offering an unparalleled glimpse into his appearance at the time of his death.

The Lindow Man met a violent and unsettling end. His throat had been slit, and he suffered blows to the head. The manner of his death, complete with ligature marks on his neck, suggests that he was strangled and then dispatched with a sharp instrument.

The motives behind his death remain shrouded in mystery. Some theories propose that he was a ritual sacrifice, while others suggest that he may have been a criminal who met his punishment.

The Lindow Man's preserved remains have provided valuable insights into his life. His well-manicured nails and lack of significant calluses on his hands suggest that he was not engaged

in heavy manual labor. His body displayed signs of physical fitness, indicating a robust lifestyle.
The absence of clothing suggests that he may have been naked or only partially dressed at the time of his death. This detail has led some experts to speculate about the ritualistic nature of his sacrifice.

The Tollund Man: Denmark's Silent Witness

The Tollund Man, discovered in Denmark's Tollund Bog in 1950, is another iconic bog body. He lived around 400 BCE, during the Iron Age. Like the Lindow Man, the Tollund Man's preservation in the peat bog is astonishing.
His hair, face, and skin were remarkably intact, and his tranquil expression belies the violence of his death. His body, when found, was carefully arranged in a fetal position, a stark contrast to the Lindow Man's more contorted posture.
The Tollund Man's death, like that of the Lindow Man, was violent and deliberate. He had been hanged, and a noose made of leather strangled him. The cause of his death suggests a deliberate act of execution or sacrifice.
While the exact circumstances of his death remain uncertain, his well-preserved body and the manner in which he was found raise intriguing questions about the significance of his demise.
The Tollund Man's physical condition provides intriguing clues about his life. He had strong arms and was in good health at the time of his death. His excellent dental health, with well-worn teeth, suggests a diet consistent with the time and region.
The Tollund Man's clothing also survived remarkably well. He wore a cap made of sheepskin and a woven leather belt, offering valuable insights into Iron Age clothing and fashion.

Parallels and Contrasts

Both the Lindow Man and the Tollund Man met violent and unnatural ends. Their deaths involved strangulation, suggesting deliberate acts of execution or sacrifice. The circumstances surrounding their deaths remain enigmatic, shrouded in the mysteries of ancient rituals or societal practices.

The preservation of both bog bodies is nothing short of astonishing. Their skin, hair, and even subtle details like stubble are remarkably intact, providing a vivid glimpse into their appearances at the time of their deaths. The unique conditions of peat bogs, characterised by low oxygen levels and acidic water, played a crucial role in this extraordinary preservation.

The positioning of the bodies is a point of contrast. The Lindow Man's contorted posture and the absence of clothing suggest a more violent and potentially ritualistic death. In contrast, the Tollund Man's carefully arranged fetal position and well-preserved clothing evoke a sense of deliberate ritual significance.

Time and Culture

The Lindow Man and the Tollund Man lived in different times and cultural contexts. The Lindow Man hails from the early Roman period in England, while the Tollund Man lived during the Iron Age in Denmark. Their lives spanned distinct epochs, marked by varying social, religious, and cultural practices.

The motives behind their deaths remain open to interpretation. The Lindow Man's death may have been related to religious or societal rituals, possibly as a form of appeasement or purification. The Tollund Man's arranged position and attire may suggest a similar ritual significance, possibly related to beliefs or practices of the Iron Age people.

The Broader Picture

The stories of the Lindow Man and the Tollund Man are just two among many bog bodies and natural mummies that have been discovered around the world. These preserved remains offer invaluable insights into the lives, deaths, and cultures of ancient societies.

The preservation of these bodies is not merely a testament to the unique conditions of peat bogs but also a testament to the enduring power of human curiosity and the quest to unravel the mysteries of our past. As researchers continue to study and analyse these ancient relics, new revelations and interpretations emerge, adding to our understanding of the enigmatic and multifaceted tapestry of human history.

"There will be time enough for sleeping in the grave."
- Benjamin Franklin

The Bone Wars - Marsh vs. Cope

In the late 19th century, the American West witnessed a scientific feud unlike any other in the history of palaeontology. This epic rivalry between two prominent palaeontologists, Othniel Charles Marsh and Edward Drinker Cope, became famously known as the "Bone Wars." Their fierce competition to discover, describe, and name new dinosaur fossils not only revolutionised the field of palaeontology but also left a legacy of scientific discovery, controversy, and enduring fascination.

Marsh: The Yale Professor

Othniel Charles Marsh, born in 1831, was a Yale University professor with a strong background in geology. Marsh had the advantage of financial support from his wealthy uncle, George Peabody, which allowed him to fund numerous fossil-hunting expeditions in the American West. His quest for fossils was driven by a desire to expand the collections at Yale's Peabody Museum of Natural History.

Cope: The Self-Taught Scholar

Edward Drinker Cope, born in 1840, was a self-taught palaeontologist and comparative anatomist. He came from a wealthy Quaker family and had a strong interest in natural history from an early age. Cope's determination and ambition led him to publish scientific papers on fossils before he had even completed his formal education.

A Race for Discovery

The Bone Wars began with a misunderstanding and a case of mistaken identity. In 1868, Cope received a shipment of fossils from Kansas, including a partial plesiosaur skeleton. In his haste to describe it, he mistakenly placed the head at the wrong end of the creature's long neck, creating a bizarre-looking "Elasmosaurus."

When Marsh saw Cope's reconstruction, he immediately recognised the error and publicly ridiculed Cope for the mistake. This incident ignited the rivalry between the two palaeontologists.

A Frenzied Competition

From that point forward, Marsh and Cope engaged in a relentless race to outdo each other in discovering, describing, and naming new dinosaur fossils. Their competition knew no bounds, and they employed various tactics to gain an advantage:

1. Hiring Fossil Hunters
Both Marsh and Cope hired teams of fossil hunters, offering them financial incentives for each significant discovery. These hunters scoured the American West, often working in challenging and perilous conditions.

2. Espionage and Sabotage
Espionage became a common practice. Each palaeontologist tried to gain information about the other's findings and planned expeditions. There were instances of fossil hunters switching allegiances or stealing valuable fossils from rival camps.

3. Hasty Descriptions
To claim priority for discoveries, Marsh and Cope often rushed to publish their findings without thorough examination or study. This sometimes led to inaccuracies and errors in their descriptions.

4. Duelling Papers
Both scientists frequently engaged in publishing wars, releasing a flurry of papers to establish their dominance in the field. This resulted in an enormous volume of scientific literature during the Bone Wars era.

The Impact on Science

Despite the sometimes unscrupulous tactics employed, the Bone Wars led to significant contributions to the field of palaeontology:

Dinosaur Discoveries

Marsh and Cope collectively described over 130 new dinosaur species, including some of the most iconic dinosaurs such as Stegosaurus, Allosaurus, and Triceratops.

Advancements in Knowledge

Their rivalry advanced the understanding of prehistoric life, including the recognition of the existence of large herbivorous and carnivorous dinosaurs and the concept of dinosaurs as a distinct group of reptiles.

Expansion of Collections

Their relentless pursuit of fossils led to the expansion of fossil collections at museums and institutions, which continue to benefit scientists and the public today.

The Personal Toll

The Bone Wars took a personal toll on Marsh and Cope, affecting their health, finances, and reputations:

Financial Drain

Both scientists spent vast sums of their own money on fossil-hunting expeditions, sometimes leading to financial ruin.

Professional Scrutiny

Their fierce competition often led to criticisms from their peers, who were concerned about the quality and accuracy of their work.

Diminished Reputations

Despite their contributions, the cutthroat nature of the rivalry tarnished the legacies of both Marsh and Cope.

Advances in Palaeontology

The Bone Wars, though marked by controversy, significantly advanced the field of palaeontology. The rivalry led to a surge in dinosaur discoveries and our understanding of prehistoric life.

The intense media coverage of the Bone Wars captivated the public's imagination and fuelled interest in palaeontology, inspiring future generations of scientists and dinosaur enthusiasts.

The legacy of Marsh and Cope lives on in the ongoing discoveries made by palaeontologists worldwide. The fossils they unearthed continue to provide valuable insights into Earth's ancient past.

Monster Maker and Organ Taker - The Wicked Works of Vladimir Demikhov

Vladimir Petrovich Demikhov was born on the 18th of July 1916, in Russia. He was a brilliant and innovative surgeon who gained international recognition for his work in organ transplantation. One of his most controversial and influential areas of research involved experiments on dogs. Demikhov's dog experiments, conducted primarily in the 1950s and 1960s, were groundbreaking but raised ethical concerns that continue to be debated today.

Early Career

Demikhov began his medical career at the Pavlov Institute of Physiology in Leningrad (now St. Petersburg), where he worked under the guidance of Ivan Petrovich Pavlov, a Nobel laureate in Physiology or Medicine. Demikhov's early research focused on the physiology of digestion and the role of the nervous system in regulating bodily functions. This foundation in physiology would later prove crucial to his pioneering work in transplantation.

One of Demikhov's most significant contributions to medical science was his development of heart-lung transplantation techniques. In the 1940s, Demikhov began experimenting with heart transplantation in dogs. His initial attempts faced many challenges, as he struggled to overcome problems related to graft rejection and the difficulties of preserving organs outside the body.

By the early 1950s, Demikhov had made significant progress. He became the first surgeon to successfully perform a heart-lung transplantation in a dog, demonstrating that it was possible to replace both the heart and lungs in a living organism. This achievement marked a major milestone in the field of transplantation and paved the way for future advancements in human organ transplantation.

The Controversial Two-Headed Dog Experiments

While Demikhov's heart-lung transplantation work garnered international attention, he is perhaps best known for his controversial two-headed dog experiments. These experiments involved grafting the head and upper body of one dog onto another dog's body, creating a two-headed creature. The goal of these experiments was to explore the possibilities of connecting the circulatory and nervous systems of two animals.

Demikhov performed a series of these surgeries in the 1950s and early 1960s, capturing the imagination of the public and the scientific community alike. The resulting two-headed dogs, though only living for a short time due to the challenges of maintaining such a complex organism, offered insights into the potential for transplanting and connecting various body parts.

Demikhov's two-headed dog experiments were met with significant ethical concerns and criticism, both in the Soviet Union and internationally. Many viewed these experiments as cruel and inhumane, raising questions about the ethical treatment of animals in scientific research. Critics argued that the suffering endured by the dogs outweighed the scientific knowledge gained.

The ethical debate surrounding Demikhov's work persists to this day. While some argue that his experiments paved the way for important advancements in transplantation and understanding the integration of organs, others maintain that the ethical cost was too high.

Impact on Organ Transplantation

Despite the ethical controversies, Demikhov's work had a lasting impact on the field of organ transplantation. His pioneering techniques and innovations in transplantation surgery laid the foundation for future breakthroughs in the field.

Demikhov's research helped refine techniques for heart transplantation and led to a better understanding of graft rejection and the importance of immunosuppressive drugs. His contributions directly influenced the first successful human heart transplant, performed by Dr. Christiaan Barnard in 1967. Furthermore, Demikhov's experiments on the transplantation of vital organs like the heart and lungs contributed to our understanding of the complexities involved in keeping transplanted organs viable and functional. This knowledge has been instrumental in improving the success rates of organ transplants in humans.

Lambs to the Slaughter- The Evil of Tuskegee

The Tuskegee Syphilis Study stands as one of the most egregious examples of ethical violations in medical research in the United States. This study, conducted over four decades from 1932 to 1972, unfolded in Macon County, Alabama, and had a profound impact on the understanding of medical ethics and the rights of research participants.

The study was initiated by the U.S. Public Health Service (PHS) and primarily aimed to investigate the natural progression of syphilis in African American men. At the time, syphilis was a major public health concern, and there was a lack of knowledge about its long-term effects, especially in untreated cases. The PHS, in collaboration with the Tuskegee Institute, recruited 600 African American men, 399 of whom had syphilis, while 201 served as a control group.

Ethical Violations

One of the most disturbing aspects of the Tuskegee Syphilis Study was the unethical treatment of its participants. The study organisers intentionally withheld treatment from the men who had syphilis, even when effective treatments like penicillin became available in the 1940s. Participants were kept in the dark about their condition and the available treatments. They were deceived into believing that they were receiving free healthcare when, in reality, they were denied the proper medical care they deserved.

This unethical behaviour continued for 40 years, resulting in the suffering and deaths of many study participants. The study organisers showed a complete disregard for the well-being and rights of these men, who were predominantly poor and illiterate.

The Eventual End

The Tuskegee Syphilis Study went largely unnoticed by the public until the early 1970s when investigative journalists exposed its unethical nature. The resulting public outrage and media scrutiny led to the study's termination in 1972. By that time, 128 of the participants had died from syphilis or related complications, and many others had suffered severe health consequences.

The Tuskegee Syphilis Study had a profound impact on the field of medical ethics and research regulations. It exposed the need for strict ethical guidelines and protections for research participants. In response to this tragedy, the U.S. government implemented comprehensive reforms to ensure that such abuses could never happen again.

The National Research Act of 1974 established the National Commission for the Protection of Human Subjects of Biomedical and Behavioral Research, which developed the Belmont Report. This report outlined the principles of ethical research involving human subjects, including informed consent, beneficence, and respect for individuals.

In the aftermath of the study's exposure, the U.S. government issued a formal apology to the survivors and their families. In 1997, President Bill Clinton issued an official apology, acknowledging the "long history of racial discrimination against African Americans" in medical research and healthcare. Furthermore, the survivors and their families were provided with compensation and access to medical treatment. The Tuskegee Health Benefit Program was established to provide medical and healthcare benefits to those affected by the study.

The incident stands clear, as one of many, as a dark period in medical history, in which the sanctity of life altogether was disregarded in the cathartic pursuit of power. It's victims, and perpetrators, act as cautionary tales for those seeking to forgo compassion and dignity in their in own lives.

Pseudosorcery - The Mad World of Alchemy

The Secret Search for a Homunculus

The Peculiar Pursuit of a Miniature Man

The term "homunculus" originates from Latin, where it means "little man." The concept of the homunculus can be traced back to ancient and medieval alchemical writings, where it was often associated with the idea of creating life artificially. These early alchemists believed that through secret rituals and magical processes, they could produce miniature human beings, often no taller than a hand's breadth, with special abilities and knowledge.

Alchemical texts from the Middle Ages contain references to the creation of homunculi using mystical recipes and ingredients. These writings described elaborate procedures that included combining semen with various substances, sealing the mixture in a container, and allowing it to incubate for a certain period. The result, it was claimed, would be a fully formed but miniature human.

These alchemical practices, while fantastical, were rooted in the alchemical pursuit of transformation and the transmutation of base materials into noble ones. The creation of a homunculus represented a symbolic goal, reflecting the alchemist's desire to unlock hidden knowledge and spiritual enlightenment.

Pragmatic Paracelsus

One of the most famous figures associated with the homunculus is the Renaissance alchemist and physician Paracelsus. While he is known for his contributions to early medicine and chemistry, Paracelsus also explored the concept of the homunculus. He proposed that a homunculus could be created by fermenting human sperm in horse manure, a bizarre notion even by the standards of the time.

In modern times, the idea of creating a homunculus has been popularised and romanticised in literature and science fiction. Prominent authors like Mary Shelley, in her novel "Frankenstein," and H.P. Lovecraft, in his work "The Dunwich Horror," have explored themes of artificial creation and the consequences of tampering with the natural order. These stories, while imaginative, underscore the ethical and moral dilemmas surrounding the concept of creating life in a laboratory.

From a scientific standpoint, the creation of a true homunculus remains firmly in the realm of fiction. The complexities of human development, genetic programming, and the intricacies of cellular biology make it impossible to craft a miniature, fully functioning human through alchemical or artificial means. While advances in genetics and reproductive technologies have allowed for cloning and manipulation of genes, the idea of creating a miniature human with a complete, autonomous consciousness remains beyond the scope of current scientific understanding and capability.

The Race for the Philosopher's Stone

The Ecstasy of Gold

The concept of the Philosopher's Stone can be traced back to ancient civilisations such as Egypt, where early alchemists sought to harness the transformative power of the gods. In these early traditions, the Stone symbolised not only material wealth but also spiritual enlightenment, bridging the divide between the physical and spiritual realms. Central to the pursuit of the Philosopher's Stone was the idea that it could transmute base metals like lead into noble ones like gold—a process known as chrysopoeia. Alchemists believed that uncovering the secrets of the Stone would lead to enlightenment and mastery over both the material and spiritual worlds. This quest became a central focus of alchemical studies throughout the Middle Ages and the Renaissance.

Alchemy in the Middle Ages

The medieval and Renaissance periods witnessed a surge in alchemical activity in Europe, with many prominent figures engaging in the quest for the Philosopher's Stone. Notable alchemists like Paracelsus and Nicolas Flamel dedicated their lives to uncovering the secrets of alchemy. Flamel, in particular, was renowned for his supposed discovery of the Philosopher's Stone, although the veracity of his claims remains a subject of debate.

The pursuit of the Philosopher's Stone was not just about material transformation. It was also deeply symbolic and mystical. Alchemical texts and symbols, filled with allegory and metaphor, represented the spiritual journey of the alchemist as they sought enlightenment and personal transformation. The stages of alchemical transformation, from the nigredo (blackness) to the albedo (whiteness) and finally to the rubedo (redness), mirrored the inner journey of the alchemist's soul.

Sorcerous Scientists

Paradoxically, while the quest for the Philosopher's Stone was steeped in mysticism, alchemists made significant contributions to early chemistry and scientific understanding. Their experiments with distillation, metallurgy, and the development of laboratory equipment laid the groundwork for modern chemistry. While the goal of transmuting base metals into gold remained elusive, alchemy played a pivotal role in the development of the scientific method.

"Live, and be happy, and make others so..."
- Mary Shelley
(Frankenstein)

Lofty Ambitions - A Brief History of Early Aviation

It is the very nature of mankind to yearn for more. Since we could walk, we have wished to run. Since we could run, we have wished to climb. And since we could climb, we have wished to fly.

One Small Flight for Man

The story of the hot air balloon's invention revolves around the pioneering spirit of two French brothers, Joseph-Michel and Jacques-Étienne Montgolfier. In 1782, they stumbled upon a phenomenon that would change the course of history - the discovery that hot air could lift objects. They witnessed this phenomenon when a piece of paper suspended over a fire was lifted into the air. This simple observation ignited their curiosity and led to the creation of the world's first hot air balloon.

In June 1783, the Montgolfier brothers constructed a large, linen-lined paper balloon and filled it with hot air from a fire below. To the amazement of onlookers in the town of Annonay, France, the balloon soared upwards, marking the birth of human flight. News of this incredible feat spread like wildfire, captivating the imagination of people across Europe.

Just a few months later, in September 1783, the Montgolfier brothers made history once again. This time, they sent a larger, more elaborate balloon with passengers, including a sheep, a duck, and a rooster, on an untethered flight in Versailles. The flight was a resounding success, and it demonstrated that living beings could safely ascend into the skies.

The hot air balloon quickly gained popularity as a symbol of human achievement and adventure. In 1785, the first human passengers, Jean-François Pilâtre de Rozier and François Laurent d'Arbaud, took to the skies in a tethered flight, ushering in the era of manned hot air ballooning.

Air Force '63

The hot air balloon saw extensive use by the Union during the troubled days of the American Civil War. The long-range flight (relatively speaking) of the aerial crafts, coupled with their versatility over various landscapes, made them exceptional choices for surveillance. Fitted with rudimentary camera equipment, the balloons acted as invisible, inaudible, and intangible spies behind Confederate lines. The success of the novel approach would soon lead to another major chapter in aviation.

Aluminium Juggernauts

The invention of the zeppelin marked another significant milestone in the history of aviation, offering a new dimension to air travel and exploration. The zeppelin, named after its creator Count Ferdinand von Zeppelin, was a rigid, cigar-shaped airship that combined the principles of hot air balloons with innovative engineering.

Count Ferdinand von Zeppelin, a retired German army officer, became captivated by the idea of air travel during the American Civil War, where he observed the potential of balloons for reconnaissance purposes. Inspired by this, he began working on his airship design in the late 19th century, overcoming numerous setbacks and challenges.

The key innovation in the zeppelin's design was the use of a rigid aluminium framework, which provided structural stability and allowed for greater control and manoeuvrability compared to earlier non-rigid balloons. Inside this framework, a series of gas-filled cells, usually filled with hydrogen due to its buoyancy, provided lift.

The first successful flight of a zeppelin took place on July 2, 1900, when Zeppelin's LZ1 lifted off the ground in Germany. Although this maiden voyage was relatively short, covering only 5.6 miles, it marked the beginning of a new era in aviation.

The potential applications of zeppelins were diverse. They were used for passenger transportation, military reconnaissance, and even as floating platforms for scientific research and advertising. One of the most famous zeppelins, the LZ 127 Graf Zeppelin, completed the first round-the-world airship voyage in 1929, showcasing the global reach of this technology.

However, the use of highly flammable hydrogen gas as a lifting agent posed a significant safety risk. This was tragically illustrated by the infamous Hindenburg disaster in 1937 when the LZ 129 Hindenburg, a passenger airship, caught fire while attempting to land in Lakehurst, New Jersey. This disaster marked a turning point in the history of airships and hastened the transition to non-flammable helium gas for lift.

Chapter Five

Unusual Customs and Tall Tales

Bizarre Historical Funeral Customs - A Grave Matter

Death is a universal human experience, and the way we bid farewell to the departed has taken on countless forms throughout history. From solemn ceremonies to downright bizarre rituals, this chapter takes you on a journey through some of the most peculiar funeral customs that humans have ever concocted. Brace yourself!

Self-Flagellation at Funerals

Let's begin our tour of the bizarre with a practice that might make you raise an eyebrow or two: self-flagellation at funerals. In certain cultures, mourners would express their grief by whipping themselves with thorny branches or other instruments of self-inflicted pain. The idea was to show the depth of their sorrow and remorse for not having prevented the death. Call it devotion, call it peculiar, but it was certainly a memorable way to mourn.

The Funeral Strippers of Taiwan

Fast-forward to modern times, and you might stumble upon a Taiwanese funeral that features something decidedly unconventional: strippers. Yes, you read that correctly. In some Taiwanese communities, particularly in rural areas, it has become a tradition to hire scantily clad dancers to perform at funerals.

The rationale behind this unusual custom is twofold: it's believed to ensure a large turnout at the funeral (who would want to miss such an event?), and it's thought to help appease wandering spirits by providing them with a memorable send-off. Whether or not this tradition achieves its intended goals is up for debate, but it's certainly a funeral experience that's hard to forget.

Death by 1000 Cuts - The Sky Burials of Tibet

Now, let's take a journey to the picturesque and mystic land of Tibet, where death is met with an entirely different approach. In a practice known as a "sky burial," the deceased is dismembered and left on a mountaintop to be devoured by vultures.

While this might sound like something out of a horror film, it's actually a deeply spiritual ritual in Tibetan Buddhism. The belief is that by offering their bodies to the birds, the deceased are aiding in the cycle of life and death. It's certainly not for the faint of heart, but it's a reminder that cultural perspectives on death can be as diverse as the landscapes they come from.

Famadihana - The Turning of the Bones in Madagascar

In Madagascar, they celebrate death with a ceremony that might be described as a joyful, albeit strange, dance with the departed. Known as Famadihana, or the "Turning of the Bones," this custom involves exhuming the bodies of deceased relatives and rewrapping them in fresh burial cloths. Family members then dance with the rewrapped bodies to live music. This celebration is rooted in the belief that the spirits of the deceased remain with the living and that through Famadihana, the living can express their enduring love and connection. While it may seem unusual to Western sensibilities, it's a touching way for families to remember and honour their ancestors.

The Festival of the Dead in Mexico

If you ever find yourself in Mexico around late October, you'll encounter a unique blend of spooky and sentimental as the country celebrates Dia de los Muertos, or the Day of the Dead. It's a lively and vibrant festival that honours deceased loved ones with altars, marigold flowers, and sugar skulls.

Perhaps the quirkiest element of this tradition is the practice of creating small, edible sugar skulls adorned with the names of the living and the deceased. Families gather to enjoy meals and share stories at the graves of their loved ones. It's a celebration of life and death that beautifully combines solemnity with a touch of whimsy.

The Whispering Death - The Torajan Funeral Ritual

In the Toraja region of Indonesia, death is an ongoing dialogue with the deceased. In a unique and somewhat eerie custom, the Torajans often keep the bodies of the deceased in their homes for weeks, months, or even years after death. During this time, the living interact with the dead, speaking to them, feeding them, and even taking them for walks.

The belief is that the soul of the deceased remains connected to their body, and only after a prolonged period does the spirit truly depart. It's a reminder that cultural perspectives on death and the afterlife can vary widely, and what might seem eerie to some is deeply meaningful to others.

The Posthumous Wedding in France

Imagine getting married to someone who has already departed this world. In certain parts of France, this surreal scenario became a reality in the 19th century. Known as "posthumous weddings," these unions occurred when one of the betrothed passed away before the wedding could take place.

In such cases, the living would marry a symbolic representation of their deceased partner, often a photograph or a mannequin dressed in wedding attire. It was believed that this practice helped resolve any unfinished business and provide closure to the grieving partner. While it might seem bizarre, it's a testament to the power of love and the lengths people will go to find solace in their grief.

The Coffin-Sitters of Ghana

In Ghana, some communities have a custom that's a mix of reverence and the supernatural. When a person of importance passes away, they are sometimes buried in a custom-designed coffin that reflects their occupation or passion in life. For instance, a fisherman might be laid to rest in a coffin shaped like a fish, or a teacher in one shaped like a book.

But what truly makes this practice unique is the inclusion of professional mourners known as "coffin-sitters." These individuals are hired to sit atop the coffins and engage in lively performances, singing and dancing to celebrate the life of the departed. It's a colourful and joyful way to bid farewell to loved ones, and it adds a touch of theatricality to the grieving process.

The Burial Beads of South Korea

In South Korea, there's an eco-friendly way to commemorate the deceased while protecting the environment: burial beads. Rather than traditional burials that consume valuable land, some South Koreans opt for a more sustainable approach. The remains of the deceased are cremated, and the ashes are compressed into colourful beads.

These beads can be displayed at home or placed in a columbarium, providing a tangible and colourful tribute to the departed. It's an innovative and environmentally conscious way to honour loved ones and preserve precious land resources.

Haunted Locations - Where the Living and the Dead Collide

Prepare to step into the realm of the supernatural as we journey through some of the world's most bizarre haunted locations. From ghostly ships to cursed islands and haunted forests, these eerie places have captured the imagination of thrill-seekers and paranormal enthusiasts alike. It's a spine-tingling adventure into the unknown where the line between the living and the dead blurs.

The Ghostly Crew of the Mary Celeste

Our journey into the world of the bizarre and haunted begins on the high seas with the Mary Celeste, a ship that has captured the imaginations of sailors and storytellers for over a century. In 1872, the Mary Celeste was discovered adrift in the Atlantic Ocean, its crew mysteriously vanished without a trace.
The ship's logbook revealed no signs of distress or foul play, and all of the crew's belongings, including valuable cargo, were left untouched. To this day, the fate of the Mary Celeste remains a mystery, and it's said that the ghostly crew still roams the decks, forever searching for answers to their inexplicable disappearance.

The Cursed Island of Poveglia

Nestled in the tranquil waters of the Venetian Lagoon lies the island of Poveglia, a place that has earned a chilling reputation as one of the most haunted locations in Italy. Throughout history, Poveglia served as a quarantine station for plague-stricken individuals, and its soil is said to contain the remains of thousands who perished during outbreaks.
The island's dark history doesn't end there. In the early 20th century, it was home to a mental institution where patients reportedly endured horrific treatments. Today, Poveglia is abandoned and off-limits to the public, but tales of ghostly

encounters and restless spirits persist. It's a place where the tortured souls of the past continue to haunt the living.

The Enchanted Forest of Hoia Baciu

Venture into the heart of Transylvania, and you'll find the Hoia Baciu Forest, a place where nature's beauty collides with the paranormal. This forest is renowned for its strange occurrences, including inexplicable electronic malfunctions, sightings of UFOs, and encounters with shadowy figures.

The most famous phenomenon in the Hoia Baciu Forest is the "Circle of Trees," where nothing grows, and the trees are twisted into unnatural shapes. Locals and visitors have reported feelings of dread, nausea, and disorientation when venturing into this eerie clearing. It's a place where the boundary between the natural world and the supernatural is blurred.

The Mystery of the Winchester Mystery House

In San Jose, California, stands a mansion with a peculiar history that has baffled visitors and paranormal investigators alike. The Winchester Mystery House, built by Sarah Winchester, the widow of the inventor of the Winchester rifle, is a labyrinthine mansion filled with staircases that lead to nowhere, doors that open into walls, and secret passages.

Legend has it that Sarah Winchester believed she was haunted by the spirits of those killed by the rifles her husband's company manufactured. To appease these restless souls, she continuously built and renovated the house, believing that construction would confuse the spirits. Today, the mansion is a popular tourist attraction, and many claim to have encountered the ghostly presence of Sarah Winchester herself.

The Château de Brissac - Home to the Green Lady

In the heart of France's Loire Valley stands the Château de Brissac, a picturesque castle with a dark secret. This 15th-century castle is home to the Green Lady, a ghostly apparition

said to be the spirit of Charlotte of France, a former resident who met a tragic end.
The story goes that Charlotte was murdered by her husband, who caught her in an affair. Her ghost is said to roam the halls of the castle, dressed in green, and her eerie presence has been witnessed by many visitors. The Green Lady is a reminder that even the most beautiful of places can conceal a haunting past.

The Screaming Bridge of Overtoun
In the Scottish town of Dumbarton, there's a bridge that has earned a chilling reputation as the "Screaming Bridge." The Overtoun Bridge, built in the 19th century, has witnessed an unusually high number of dogs leaping to their deaths.
Local legend has it that the bridge is haunted by the ghost of Lady Overtoun, who is said to have tragically lost her child near the bridge. Some believe that her restless spirit lures dogs to their deaths, while others point to unusual smells or sounds that may attract the animals. The mystery of the Overtoun Bridge remains unsolved, but it serves as a haunting reminder of the unexplained.

The Ghostly Residents of the Tower of London
No list of haunted locations would be complete without mentioning the Tower of London, a historic fortress with a storied past. The Tower is said to be haunted by a slew of ghostly residents, including Anne Boleyn, the ill-fated wife of Henry VIII, and Lady Jane Grey, who was executed there.
One of the Tower's most famous apparitions is the "White Lady," believed to be the spirit of Arbella Stuart, who died in captivity. Visitors and guards have reported eerie encounters and unexplained phenomena within the Tower's walls. It's a place where history and the supernatural coexist in eerie harmony.

The Forbidden City of Beijing

In the heart of Beijing lies the Forbidden City, a sprawling imperial palace complex that served as the seat of power for Chinese emperors for centuries. While it may seem like a place of grandeur and history, it's also known for its eerie legends and hauntings.

The Forbidden City is said to be home to the ghost of Wanli, a Ming Dynasty emperor, who is believed to wander the halls of the palace. Visitors and guards have reported hearing footsteps and seeing apparitions within the palace walls. It's a reminder that even the most opulent of places can have a hidden, supernatural side.

"The sad intangible who grieve and yearn..."
- T.S. Elliot

Superstitions from Around the World - When Belief Defies Logic

Superstitions, those curious beliefs that defy logic and reason, are a testament to the human capacity for both ingenuity and irrationality. From lucky charms to jinxed numbers, every culture has its own peculiar set of superstitions that have been passed down through generations.

The Curse of the Number 4 in China

In many cultures, the number 4 is considered unlucky due to its phonetic similarity to the word for "death." Nowhere is this superstition more prevalent than in China. The fear of the number 4, known as tetraphobia, has led to all sorts of quirks and peculiarities.
In Chinese buildings, you'll often find the fourth floor mysteriously missing, and license plates with the number 4 are avoided like the plague. It's a superstition that permeates daily life, impacting everything from housing to hospital rooms. For the superstitious, the mere sight of the number 4 can send shivers down the spine.

The Lucky Number 7 Worldwide

On the opposite end of the numerical spectrum, we find the universally celebrated number 7. This digit has long been regarded as a symbol of luck and good fortune in cultures around the world.
From the seven wonders of the world to the seven days of the week, the number 7 pops up in countless facets of life. Even the most skeptical among us might find themselves feeling a bit luckier on the seventh day or seeking out the seventh leaf on a four-leaf clover.

The Unlucky Number 13 - A Global Phobia

While 7 basks in its glory as the lucky number, 13 stands as its equally renowned counterpart in the world of superstition. Fear of the number 13, known as triskaidekaphobia, transcends borders and cultures, resulting in all sorts of peculiar practices. Friday the 13th is perhaps the most famous example of this superstition, with many people avoiding travel or significant decisions on this ominous date. Buildings often skip the 13th floor, labelling it as 14 instead. It's a superstition that has spawned countless tales of bad luck and misfortune, even though logic tells us that numbers themselves can't bring ill fortune.

The Dreaded Broken Mirror in Western Cultures

In Western cultures, a broken mirror is often met with a sense of foreboding. The superstition goes that a broken mirror not only brings seven years of bad luck but also shatters one's soul, as the reflection in the mirror was once believed to hold a part of the person's soul.

As a result, shattered mirrors are handled with caution and even a tinge of fear. While it might be tempting to dismiss this superstition as mere irrationality, it's a reminder of the significance we attach to mirrors and our own reflections.

The Curse of the Evil Eye in Mediterranean Cultures

The concept of the evil eye is a superstition deeply ingrained in Mediterranean cultures, from Greece to Turkey to Italy. The evil eye is believed to be a malevolent gaze that can bring harm or misfortune to the recipient.

To ward off this curse, people wear charms, known as nazar or "evil eye" beads, as protective talismans. These blue and white beads are often hung in homes, cars, and even on jewellery to deflect the evil eye's harmful intentions. It's a superstition that serves as a fascinating blend of belief and symbolism, offering protection from the unseen forces of jealousy and envy.

The Lucky Horseshoe in Western Folklore
In Western folklore, the horseshoe takes on a role as a powerful symbol of luck and protection. The belief is that hanging a horseshoe above a doorway will bring good fortune to those who pass beneath it, while also warding off evil spirits. This superstition traces its origins to ancient Europe when iron was believed to have protective qualities. While it might seem like a quaint tradition, it's a reminder of the enduring power of symbols in shaping our beliefs and actions.

The Knock on Wood Tradition
Have you ever caught yourself saying, "Knock on wood," after making a hopeful statement? This quirky superstition is widespread in Western cultures and involves knocking on wood to ward off bad luck or to ensure that a positive statement remains true.
The origins of this tradition are somewhat unclear, but it's thought to stem from the belief that spirits and supernatural beings inhabit trees. Knocking on wood was a way to seek their protection or appease them when discussing positive events or good fortune. It's a superstition that has become so ingrained in our language and behaviour that we often do it without thinking.

The Curse of the Black Cat
In many cultures, black cats have been associated with bad luck and superstition. In medieval Europe, black cats were often linked to witches and were believed to bring misfortune to anyone who crossed their path.
The superstition persists today, leading some people to avoid black cats or view them with suspicion, especially around Halloween. This belief serves as a reminder of how easily animals, even those as innocuous as cats, can become entangled in human superstitions and fears.

The Red String of Fate in Eastern Beliefs
In various Asian cultures, there's a superstition known as the "Red String of Fate." It's the belief that an invisible red thread connects people who are destined to meet, regardless of time, place, or circumstances.
The red thread is said to be tied to one's pinky finger and is believed to lead individuals to their soulmates or destined friends. It's a superstition that highlights the enduring human desire to find meaning and connection in the complexities of fate and destiny.

The Curse of the Opal
Opals, with their dazzling play of colours, have long been admired for their beauty. However, in many Western cultures, opals have also been associated with bad luck and ill fortune. The superstition surrounding opals dates back to the 19th century when a novel by Sir Walter Scott portrayed opals as unlucky gemstones. This led to a decline in the popularity of opal jewellery. To this day, some people avoid wearing opals, believing that they can bring misfortune. It's a reminder that even precious stones can become entangled in the web of superstition.

The Ritual of Throwing Salt Over the Left Shoulder
You might have witnessed someone tossing a pinch of salt over their left shoulder after spilling it. This quirky superstition stems from the belief that spilling salt is a harbinger of bad luck. By throwing salt over the left shoulder, it's thought that one can ward off evil spirits or counteract the ill fortune associated with the spilled salt.
This belief has persisted for centuries, and while it might seem whimsical, it highlights the lengths to which people will go to undo perceived bad luck.

The Knocking on Wood and Spitting Traditions in Russia
In Russia, there are two curious superstitions that have been embraced by many. The first involves knocking on wood, similar to the Western tradition, to avert misfortune. The second superstition is spitting over one's left shoulder after making a positive statement to keep it from turning sour. Both of these customs reflect the human tendency to seek protection from the unpredictable forces of fate, even through seemingly odd or ritualistic behaviours.

The Lucky Elephant in Hindu Beliefs
In Hinduism, the elephant holds special significance as a symbol of luck, wisdom, and protection. Ganesh, the elephant-headed deity, is revered as the remover of obstacles and the patron of arts and sciences.
It's common to see statues and images of elephants in Hindu households and temples, especially with their trunks raised for good luck. This superstition serves as a testament to the enduring power of symbolism and belief in shaping our lives.

The Curse of the Mummy's Tomb
Mummies, with their ancient and eerie aura, have long captured the human imagination. In Western culture, there's a superstition known as the "Curse of the Pharaohs," which suggests that disturbing the tomb of an Egyptian pharaoh will bring about misfortune or even death.
This superstition gained prominence after the discovery of King Tutankhamun's tomb in 1922, during which several individuals associated with the excavation died under mysterious circumstances. While scientific explanations attribute these deaths to natural causes, the curse of the mummy's tomb endures as a reminder of the human fascination with the supernatural.

The Ritual of Breaking a Glass at Jewish Weddings
In Jewish weddings, it's customary for the groom to break a glass underfoot at the conclusion of the ceremony. While this tradition has various interpretations, one common superstition is that the shattered glass symbolises the fragility of human relationships and the hope for a marriage that lasts as long as it would take to piece the glass back together.
It's a poignant reminder that even in moments of joy and celebration, superstition can find its place in cultural rituals and customs.

The Fascination with Full and New Moons
Throughout history, full and new moons have been a source of fascination and superstition in cultures around the world. From werewolves to lunar eclipses, these celestial events have sparked tales of transformation and the supernatural.
Some superstitions suggest that full moons bring about strange behaviour in people, leading to terms like "lunatic" derived from the Latin word for moon, "luna." Others associate lunar eclipses with omens and portents. It's a reminder of our deep-rooted connection to the cosmos and our tendency to find meaning in the movements of the celestial bodies.

The Fear of Opening an Umbrella Indoors
Many of us have been scolded for opening an umbrella indoors, but do we really know why it's considered bad luck? This superstition's origins are somewhat unclear, but one theory suggests that it stems from the practicality of avoiding accidents in confined indoor spaces.
Another theory harks back to Victorian England, where large, spring-loaded umbrellas became popular. Opening one indoors could easily lead to knocking over fragile objects or causing general chaos. Regardless of its origins, the superstition persists, and many still avoid tempting fate by refraining from opening umbrellas indoors.

The Curse of the Last Cigarette in Russia

In Russia, there's a superstition that lighting the last cigarette in a pack can bring misfortune. It's believed that by doing so, you invite bad luck or even death. As a result, many people will go to great lengths to avoid being the one to light the final cigarette.

This superstition serves as a reminder that even mundane rituals can take on deeper significance when infused with belief and fear.

The Fascination with Shooting Stars

The sight of a shooting star streaking across the night sky has long been associated with wishes and good fortune. In many cultures, people believe that if you make a wish upon a shooting star, it will come true.

This superstition reflects our enduring fascination with the cosmos and the belief that the universe itself can grant our deepest desires. It's a reminder that even in the vast expanse of space, we find ways to seek meaning and hope.

Folkloric Fiends from Around the World - Things that go Bump in the Night

The world is brimming with stories of mythical creatures that have captured the imaginations of people across cultures and generations. These creatures often defy the laws of nature and stretch the boundaries of human belief.

Kitsune - The Shape-Shifting Foxes of Japan

In the quiet, moonlit forests of Japan, there exists a creature of legends and folklore, a shape-shifting trickster known as the kitsune. These cunning beings have fascinated and mystified people for centuries, with their complex blend of beauty and deception.

The kitsune's origins are as elusive as the creatures themselves. Some believe they are messengers of the Shinto rice deity, Inari, while others see them as embodiments of fox spirits or even as revered protectors of the forest. Regardless of their origin, kitsune are undeniably an integral part of Japanese culture and mythology.

A Foxy Look

Kitsune are often depicted as foxes, and their appearance can vary. They may appear as regular foxes, distinguishable only by their characteristic white or nine-tailed variations. In their human disguise, kitsune are often portrayed as alluring women, captivating those who encounter them with their mesmerising beauty.

One of the most intriguing aspects of kitsune lore is their remarkable ability to transform. They can take on the guise of humans, animals, or even inanimate objects, using their powers to deceive and manipulate those around them. This power is often associated with their age and wisdom, with older kitsune possessing greater mastery over it.

A Love-Hate Relationship

Kitsune embody a duality that makes them both revered and feared. On one hand, they are seen as protectors of the natural world, capable of bringing fortune and prosperity to those they favour. Temples dedicated to Inari often have kitsune statues as guardians, and offerings of rice, sake, and other delicacies are made to appease them.

On the other hand, kitsune are known for their mischievous nature, delighting in pranks and trickery. They may play tricks on humans, create illusions, or lead travelers astray in the forest. This dual nature reflects the complexity of human emotions and the unpredictability of the natural world.

Many kitsune legends revolve around love and the pursuit of happiness. Some kitsune fall in love with humans and take on human form to be with them, often facing moral dilemmas and tragic consequences in their quest for love and acceptance. These stories serve as cautionary tales about the complexities of human emotions and relationships.

The Chupacabra - The Elusive Vampire of Latin America

In the remote corners of Latin America, a chilling legend has gripped the imaginations of those who reside in the countryside. This legend tells of a fearsome creature known as the Chupacabra, a name that strikes terror into the hearts of farmers and villagers alike.

The word "Chupacabra" itself gives a clue to its nature, translating to "goat-sucker" in Spanish. The creature's legend is believed to have originated in Puerto Rico in the late 20th century before spreading to other parts of Latin America and even into the United States.

Frightful Guise

Descriptions of the Chupacabra vary, but it is often depicted as a reptilian, canine, or even alien-like creature.

The Chupacabra is described as a small, bipedal creature with sharp spines or quills running down its back. It is said to have glowing red or orange eyes that emit an eerie, supernatural light. Its primary claim to infamy is its alleged penchant for attacking livestock, especially goats and chickens, and draining them of their blood.

Sightings of the Chupacabra have been reported in various Latin American countries, from Mexico to Argentina. Eyewitness accounts are often filled with fear and uncertainty, as the creature is said to strike swiftly and mysteriously, leaving behind a trail of livestock carcasses with puncture wounds and drained of blood.

The Truth Behind the Legend

While the legend of the Chupacabra continues to captivate imaginations, skepticism abounds among scientists and experts. Many of the reported livestock attacks attributed to the Chupacabra have more plausible explanations, such as predation by local wildlife or diseases. As a result, the

Chupacabra is often dismissed as a cryptid or urban legend rather than a biological reality.
Despite the skepticism, the Chupacabra remains a powerful cultural symbol in Latin America. It represents the fears of rural communities, where livestock is often the lifeblood of their livelihoods. The legend serves as a reminder of the mysteries that still lurk in the darkness, and the enduring power of folklore to capture the human imagination.
The Chupacabra, whether a real creature or a product of imagination, continues to be a source of intrigue and fear in Latin American folklore. Its elusive nature, eerie description, and the stories of livestock attacks have etched it into the cultural fabric of the region, reminding us that even in the modern age, there are mysteries that defy easy explanation.

Tikbalang - The Filipino Forest Fiend

The Tikbalang is often described as a tall, humanoid creature with the head and hooves of a horse. Its long limbs and elongated fingers are said to give it an eerie, otherworldly appearance. Despite its humanoid shape, the Tikbalang's animalistic features set it apart as a creature of the supernatural. In Filipino folklore, the Tikbalang is believed to be the guardian of the forests and mountains. It is said to protect the natural world and its inhabitants, serving as a steward of the environment. As a guardian, it is both a protector and a trickster, sometimes leading travelers astray or playing pranks on those who enter its territory.

The Law of the Jungle

To navigate the forests and mountains safely, many Filipinos adhere to certain superstitious precautions to avoid the Tikbalang's mischief. Some believe that wearing their clothing inside out or uttering prayers and chants can ward off the creature's tricks. Others advise travellers to make noise while passing through the wilderness to alert the Tikbalang to their presence, thereby gaining its favour and protection.

Friend and Foe

While the Tikbalang is often portrayed as a guardian figure, it can also be unpredictable. Some legends suggest that forming a friendship with a Tikbalang can be advantageous, as they may share their knowledge of the forest and even grant favours to those who respect their domain. However, crossing a Tikbalang or disturbing its habitat can lead to misfortune or illness.

Bunyip - An Aquatic Australian Monster

The word "Bunyip" is believed to have its origins in the Wemba-Wemba or Wergaia languages of Indigenous Australians. While its precise origins are shrouded in mystery, the Bunyip's legend likely dates back centuries, passed down through oral traditions and Dreamtime stories. Different Aboriginal communities have their own interpretations and descriptions of the creature.

Descriptions of the Bunyip vary, but it is often depicted as a large, amphibious creature, resembling a blend of different animals. Some accounts describe it as having a dog-like face, dark fur or feathers, flippers, and sharp claws. Its size ranges from relatively small to enormous, depending on the storyteller.

An Avenging Force

In Aboriginal folklore, the Bunyip is sometimes seen as a guardian spirit of the waterways. It plays a role in teaching respect for the environment and the importance of maintaining a harmonious relationship with the land. On the other hand, the Bunyip is also associated with danger and is said to be responsible for mysterious disappearances and frightening encounters.

When European settlers arrived in Australia, they encountered stories of the Bunyip from Indigenous people. These accounts, often exaggerated or misinterpreted, fuelled curiosity and fear about the mysterious creature. Early settlers sometimes attributed strange and unexplained phenomena in the wilderness to the Bunyip.

Modern Understanding

In the 21st century, as scientific understanding has advanced, the Bunyip has largely been relegated to the realm of folklore and myth. Skeptics suggest that the creature may have been inspired by sightings of native animals, such as seals, wallabies, or large birds, distorted by storytelling and imagination. Despite its ambiguity, the Bunyip continues to be a part of Australian cultural identity. It represents the enduring sense of wonder and awe that the country's untamed wilderness inspires. The Bunyip's legend serves as a reminder of the vast and often uncharted territories that still exist in Australia.

Nuckelavee - The Oceanic Abomination of the Orkneys

In the stormy waters and rugged coastlines of the Orkney Islands of Scotland, a creature of nightmarish proportions haunts the depths—the Nuckelavee. This grotesque and malevolent being is a testament to the fearsome power of the sea and the mysteries that lurk beneath its waves.
The Nuckelavee's name is derived from Orcadian dialect, and its origins can be traced back to the rich folklore of the Orkney Islands. It is often considered one of the most terrifying creatures in Scottish mythology. The creature is thought to be a blend of various sea monsters and supernatural entities, representing the destructive forces of the ocean.

Nightmares Unleashed

Descriptions of the Nuckelavee are truly horrifying. It is often depicted as a creature with a horse's head on a grotesquely humanoid body, its skin tightly adhered to its skeletal frame. Its arms are long and bony, and it has flippers instead of hands and feet. The Nuckelavee is entirely skinless, exposing raw, pulsating muscles and veins. Its breath is said to be a toxic, foul-smelling miasma.
The Nuckelavee is not merely a monstrous visage; it is believed to embody the malevolence of the sea itself. It is said to emerge from the depths during storms, bringing disaster and disease to the Orkney Islands. The creature is known to sow sickness among livestock and cause blight on crops, leading to famine and hardship for the island's inhabitants.

The Path to Safety

To protect themselves from the Nuckelavee's wrath, the people of Orkney have traditionally employed various rituals and charms. These include carving protective symbols, such as the "Mare's Nipple," onto their homes and possessions. They also recite incantations and prayers to ward off the malevolent creature.

The Nuckelavee's legend serves as a reflection of the harsh and unpredictable nature of life in the coastal regions of Scotland. It embodies the fear and respect that the sea has commanded throughout history and the deep-seated belief in the supernatural forces that can shape the fate of communities dependent on the ocean for their livelihoods.

Hodag - The Local Legend of Wisconsin

The Hodag's story begins in the late 19th century in Rhinelander, Wisconsin. It was the brainchild of local land surveyor and practical joker Eugene Shepard. In 1893, Shepard claimed to have encountered the monstrous creature in the forests near the town. His story of a fearsome, horned beast with sharp teeth and spikes running down its back captured the public's imagination.

As the legend of the Hodag grew, so did skepticism. In 1896, Shepard finally revealed that the Hodag was a hoax created with the help of props, explosives, and a vivid imagination. The creature had never truly existed. Despite the revelation, the Hodag's legend endured and became a beloved part of Wisconsin folklore.

Hometown Hero

The Hodag is described as having a peculiar appearance, featuring a horned head, glowing red eyes, sharp tusks, and a row of deadly spikes or spines along its back. It is often depicted as a fearsome and grotesque creature, a blend of various animals and mythical beings.

The Hodag's legacy lives on in Rhinelander, where it serves as a symbol of local pride and a tourist attraction. The town holds an annual Hodag festival, complete with parades, games, and Hodag-themed merchandise. It has become an endearing part of Wisconsin's cultural identity, a testament to the power of storytelling and community spirit.

Local Legacy

While the Hodag may not be a real creature, its enduring presence in Wisconsin's folklore showcases the power of storytelling and the way in which legends can shape a community's identity. It reminds us that even when the truth behind a myth is revealed, the magic of the story can continue to captivate and inspire for generations to come.

Ahuizotl - The Sinister Amazonian Predator

The Ahuizotl's name is derived from the Nahuatl language, spoken by the Aztecs. It combines "ahuiz," meaning "spine" or "thorn," with "otl," which is a diminutive suffix. This name is fitting, given the creature's most distinctive feature—a hand-like appendage at the end of its tail, adorned with sharp claws or spines.

Descriptions of the Ahuizotl vary, but it is often depicted as a creature with the body of a dog or small monkey and a sleek, waterproof coat of fur. Its most striking feature is its aforementioned tail-hand, which it uses to grasp and drown unsuspecting victims. This appendage allows the Ahuizotl to be both predator and tool-user, making it a particularly sinister figure.

Dweller in the Deep

The Ahuizotl was believed to inhabit bodies of water, including rivers, lakes, and canals. It would lie in wait for those who ventured too close to the water's edge, especially children and lone travellers. The creature's tail-hand was used to grab its prey and drag them beneath the surface to meet their demise.

In Aztec mythology, the Ahuizotl was often associated with water deities and rituals. It was seen as a symbol of the dangers lurking in the depths, a reminder of the unpredictable and sometimes treacherous nature of water. Some accounts suggest that the Ahuizotl may have been invoked in sacrificial ceremonies to appease water gods.

Yara-Ma-Ya-Who - An Outback Bloodsucker

In the timeless landscapes of Australia, the Aboriginal people have shared tales of a peculiar and unique creature known as the Yara-ma-yha-who.

The name "Yara-ma-yha-who" is derived from Aboriginal languages, with variations in pronunciation depending on the region. In Aboriginal mythology, it is often considered a mystical or supernatural creature rather than a straightforward animal. The stories surrounding the Yara-ma-yha-who have been passed down through generations, reflecting the deep spiritual connection between Aboriginal communities and their land.

Crimson Creature

The Yara-ma-yha-who is often depicted as a diminutive, red-skinned creature with a round belly and long, gangly limbs. It has an oversized head and a wide, toothless mouth, making it appear both comical and unsettling. Despite its odd appearance, it is a creature to be feared.

One of the most curious aspects of the Yara-ma-yha-who's legend is its predatory behaviour. It is said to lurk in the canopies of trees, waiting patiently for an unsuspecting traveler to pass beneath. When the opportunity arises, the creature descends silently and pounces upon its victim.

Succulent Meal

The Yara-ma-yha-who's method of predation is what truly sets it apart. Rather than devouring its prey, it prefers to suck the blood from its victim, using the suction cups on the palms of its hands and the soles of its feet. Once its meal is drained of blood, the Yara-ma-yha-who regurgitates the victim, who is left weaker but still alive. Bit by bit, this process is repeated, until the unfortunate victim becomes a new Yara-ma-ya-who themselves.

Roc - Jewel of the Skies

The earliest accounts of the Roc can be traced to Middle Eastern and South Asian mythology, particularly in Arabic, Persian, and Indian tales. This legendary bird was often described as a gigantic eagle or falcon, with wingspans so vast that they could blot out the sun.

Flights of Fancy

In the tales of Arabian Nights, the Roc was depicted as a bird capable of carrying off elephants and other large creatures. Some stories even claimed it could snatch entire ships from the sea with its talons. The imagery of such a colossal avian predator gave rise to a sense of wonder and fear among those who heard these stories.

The Roc's symbolism transcends its physical attributes. It has been seen as a representation of power, freedom, and the boundless reach of the natural world. In some cultures, it was associated with celestial themes, often serving as a messenger between the mortal realm and the heavens.

Global Wingspan

The concept of the Roc transcended geographical boundaries, making appearances in the folklore of diverse cultures. In Chinese mythology, for example, the mythical bird known as the "Zhu Feng" shares similarities with the Roc. These tales reflect humanity's fascination with the idea of a colossal, majestic bird.

The Roc's influence extended beyond folklore. It made its mark in literature, with writers like Edgar Allan Poe referencing it in their works. In art, depictions of the Roc adorned manuscripts, paintings, and sculptures, contributing to the rich tapestry of mythological creatures.

The Loveland Frog - One of the Strangest Beasts in Ohio

The story of the Loveland Frog begins in the early hours of a summer night in 1955. A businessman driving along an isolated stretch of road spotted three bizarre, frog-like creatures. Standing upright at about 3 to 4 feet tall, they had leathery skin and webbed hands and feet. The most striking detail was their distinctive, human-like faces, complete with wide eyes and expressive mouths.

Growing Discontent

Over the years, reports of Loveland Frog sightings have emerged sporadically. Witnesses claim to have seen these unusual creatures near bridges, roadsides, and the banks of the river. While some encounters are met with skepticism, others insist on the authenticity of their experiences.

As with many urban legends, rational explanations have been offered for the Loveland Frog sightings. Some suggest that misidentified wildlife, such as large iguanas or escaped exotic pets, could account for the mysterious creatures. Others believe that the stories may have been influenced by the popular culture of the time, including science fiction and horror movies.

Slimy Legacy

The Loveland Frog has become an integral part of local folklore, with its image appearing on murals, in festivals, and even as a mascot for Loveland's minor league baseball team. It has also captured the imagination of cryptid enthusiasts and paranormal investigators who continue to search for evidence of its existence.

"Mr Holmes, they were the footprints of a gigantic hound!"
- Sir Arthur Conan Doyle (The Hound of the Baskervilles)

The Dancing Plague of 1518 - A Dance to the Edge of Insanity

Few events are as bizarre and perplexing as the Dancing Plague of 1518. This strange phenomenon, which gripped the town of Strasbourg, France, defies conventional explanation, leaving behind a haunting and enigmatic legacy that continues to perplex historians and scientists to this day.

The Mysterious Outbreak

The year was 1518, and Strasbourg, a bustling town in Alsace, France, was about to become the epicentre of an inexplicable and macabre event. It all began in July when a woman known as Frau Troffea took to the streets and began to dance. Her movements were frenetic and uncontrolled, and she showed no signs of stopping.

The Dance That Wouldn't End

Days turned into weeks, and Frau Troffea's solitary dance continued unabated. She danced until her feet were bloodied and blistered, yet she could not be persuaded to stop. Instead, her strange performance attracted a growing crowd of onlookers.
But Frau Troffea was not alone for long. Within a month, more than 30 people had joined her in this bizarre dance marathon. They twirled and gyrated with seemingly boundless energy, and their numbers continued to swell.

The Spreading Hysteria

As the Dancing Plague spread through Strasbourg, it began to take on a life of its own. The afflicted individuals showed no signs of joy or celebration; instead, they appeared tormented and pained by their ceaseless dancing. Many were drenched in sweat, their faces contorted with anguish.

Local authorities, baffled by the situation, initially assumed that the dancers were suffering from a kind of "hot blood" and that the only way to cure them was to let them dance until the affliction passed. They even went so far as to organise musicians and a wooden stage to accommodate the growing number of dancers.

The Height of Hysteria

By August of 1518, the Dancing Plague had reached its zenith. The streets of Strasbourg were filled with dancers, many of whom had danced themselves to the point of exhaustion and collapse. Some danced until they suffered heart attacks or strokes, and a number of them died from sheer physical exertion.

Witnesses described the dancers as being in a trance-like state, unable to control their movements or stop dancing, no matter how dire the consequences. The spectacle was both tragic and bewildering.

Medical and Mystical Explanations

As the Dancing Plague persisted, various theories emerged to explain the inexplicable. Physicians of the time speculated that the dancing was the result of "hot blood," an imbalance of bodily humours. Some believed that the afflicted individuals needed to be purged of this excess heat through dancing.

Others turned to supernatural explanations. Some believed that the dancers were possessed by demons or that they had incurred the wrath of Saint Vitus, a Christian martyr associated with dancing. It was even suggested that the dancers might find relief by visiting the shrine of Saint Vitus.

The Unanswered Questions

To this day, the Dancing Plague of 1518 remains a mystery. What could have driven so many people to dance uncontrollably, even to the point of death? Was it a mass psychogenic illness, a form of mass hysteria that spread through suggestion and fear?

The Dancing Plague of 1518 eventually subsided, leaving Strasbourg with a lingering sense of unease and bewilderment. But the incident did not fade into obscurity. Instead, it became a historical enigma, a subject of fascination and speculation for generations to come.

Possible Explanations

While the exact cause of the Dancing Plague remains uncertain, modern scholars have put forth several theories to explain this peculiar event:

Mass Psychogenic Illness

One prevailing theory is that the Dancing Plague was a form of mass psychogenic illness, also known as mass hysteria. In situations of extreme stress or anxiety, individuals can be susceptible to psychological contagion, leading to symptoms that manifest as a physical response, such as uncontrollable dancing.

Ergot Poisoning

Another hypothesis is that the dancers may have consumed rye bread contaminated with ergot, a fungus that can produce hallucinations, spasms, and other neurological symptoms. Ergot poisoning can lead to altered states of consciousness and erratic behaviour, which could explain the frenetic dancing.

Deadly Fashion Trends - Dressing to Kill in the 19th Century

The 19th century was an era of exquisite fashion and societal norms, where appearance often took precedence over practicality. In the quest for beauty, some of the garments and accessories of this period concealed a dark and dangerous secret. From dazzling gowns to stunning hats, these fashion choices harboured hidden toxins that, unbeknownst to many, posed significant health risks.

Eyes Green with Envy

In the realm of colours, green has always held a special fascination for humans. It represents life, growth, and nature's abundant beauty. Yet, lurking behind the vibrant allure of green, there lies a darker tale - the story of Paris green, a pigment that played a notorious role in history as both an artist's tool and a deadly poison.

The history of Paris green begins in the 18th century when the desire for a vivid green pigment led to various experiments by chemists and artists. Prior to its discovery, green pigments were often derived from toxic substances like arsenic, which had health hazards for those who used them.

In 1775, a Swedish chemist named Carl Wilhelm Scheele stumbled upon a new formulation. He combined copper arsenite and acetic acid, resulting in a brilliant green pigment. This pigment came to be known as "Schweinfurt green" after the German town where it was first mass-produced. Later, it became more widely recognised as "Paris green" due to its use in France.

Paris green quickly gained popularity among artists, particularly in the 19th century. Its vivid hue allowed painters to create lush landscapes and vibrant still-life compositions. Impressionist painters like Claude Monet and Camille Pissarro utilised Paris green to capture the essence of nature in their works.

However, the artists who wielded this pigment were often unaware of its toxic nature. Handling Paris green could lead to skin irritations, and inhaling its dust or fumes could result in severe health problems. It was a dark irony that the very colour symbolising life and nature concealed a deadly secret.
The hidden dangers of Paris green became more apparent outside the realm of art. It found its way into various applications beyond the canvas. In the 19th century, Paris green was used as an insecticide to combat pests in agriculture. Sprayed on crops to ward off insects, it was effective but also posed serious risks to both farmworkers and consumers.
The poisonous effects of Paris green came to the forefront when cases of illness and death were linked to its use. This led to increasing awareness of its dangers, and eventually, its use as an insecticide was phased out in favour of safer alternatives.

As Mad as a Hatter

The story of mercury in hat making can be traced back to the late 17th century. Hatters, the skilled artisans responsible for crafting hats, were constantly seeking ways to improve the appearance and durability of their products. They discovered that treating fur, often rabbit or beaver fur, with a solution containing mercuric nitrate produced a unique effect. The fur took on a glossy, metallic sheen that was highly desirable at the time.

This technique led to the creation of "beaver hats" or "mercury hats," which became incredibly fashionable in the 18th century. These hats were favoured by the aristocracy and the upper classes, symbolising wealth and sophistication.

What hat wearers and hatters of the time didn't fully comprehend was the perilous nature of the mercury-infused fur. Mercury, a highly toxic heavy metal, was being absorbed through the skin and inhaled as hatters worked with the treated fur. The consequences of chronic mercury exposure soon became apparent.

Hatters began to exhibit a range of symptoms, including tremors, mood swings, and cognitive decline. These ailments gave rise to the colloquial phrase "mad as a hatter," which later inspired Lewis Carroll's portrayal of the Mad Hatter in "Alice's Adventures in Wonderland." In reality, hatters were indeed suffering from mercury poisoning.

As the dangers of mercury exposure became more widely known, regulations were put in place to protect workers in the hat-making industry. In the 19th century, countries like England and the United States enacted laws to limit the use of mercury in hat production. This led to the decline of the mercury hat and the rise of alternative methods for achieving a glossy finish on fur.

A Hot Mess

While the Victorian era was known for its elaborate and luxurious clothing, many of these garments were made from highly flammable materials such as silk, tulle, and lace. The popularity of these fabrics was driven by their exquisite appearance and the status they conveyed.

Silk, in particular, was a favoured choice for gowns and accessories. Its shimmering texture and ability to hold vibrant dyes made it highly desirable. However, silk was notorious for its flammability, and incidents of clothing catching fire were not uncommon.

The danger of wearing flammable fabrics in the 19th century was compounded by the widespread use of candles, oil lamps, and open flames for illumination. Ballrooms and social gatherings were often lit by chandeliers with real candles, creating an environment ripe for potential disasters.

To mitigate the risks, some fashion-conscious individuals wore fire-resistant undergarments or took precautions by avoiding open flames when wearing their extravagant attire. Nonetheless, the allure of silk, lace, and tulle persisted, and the fashion world continued to grapple with the delicate balance between beauty and safety in clothing.

If Looks Could Kill

The 19th century witnessed a catastrophic toll on wildlife driven by the insatiable demand for fashionable accessories and garments. This era was marked by an extravagant obsession with exotic animal products, resulting in the widespread destruction of countless species and ecosystems.

One of the most glaring examples of this ecological devastation was the rampant poaching of animals for their skins, feathers, and furs. Birds such as egrets, herons, and birds of paradise were hunted to the brink of extinction for their plumes, which adorned the elaborate hats and clothing of the fashionable elite. The relentless pursuit of these avian treasures decimated entire bird populations and disrupted fragile ecosystems.

Another devastating consequence of 19th-century fashion was the demand for fur, which led to the near-extinction of various mammal species. Beaver, otter, and mink were prized for their soft and luxurious fur, while seals faced brutal harvesting for their pelts. In pursuit of these coveted materials, hunters and trappers often engaged in unsustainable practices, endangering entire animal species.

Exotic leather goods, such as those made from the skins of snakes, crocodiles, and big cats, also became highly sought after. The relentless harvesting of these animals not only posed a grave threat to their survival but also disrupted the balance of ecosystems in their native habitats.

The destructive impact of 19th-century fashion on wildlife eventually sparked early conservation efforts and led to the establishment of wildlife protection laws. Pioneers like Audubon and the founding of organisations like the Audubon Society were instrumental in raising awareness about the devastating consequences of fashion's obsession with exotic animal products.

In hindsight, the 19th century serves as a stark reminder of the dire consequences that can result from unchecked consumerism and a lack of environmental awareness. The destruction of wildlife during this era underscores the importance of sustainable fashion practices and conservation efforts in the modern world to protect our fragile ecosystems and preserve the planet's biodiversity.

"Don't make fashion own you."
- Gianni Versace

The Mystery of the Lead Masks of Vintem Hill

Nestled in the hills surrounding Rio de Janeiro, Brazil, lies a place that harbours one of the most perplexing mysteries of the 20th century - the Lead Masks of Vintem Hill. This enigmatic story, shrouded in obscurity and intrigue, has baffled investigators and conspiracy theorists for decades, offering more questions than answers.

The Discovery

The tale begins on August 20, 1966, when a young boy flying his kite stumbled upon two lifeless bodies atop Vintem Hill. What would have been a routine discovery of an unfortunate accident soon took an eerie turn. The bodies of Manoel Pereira da Cruz and Miguel José Viana, two electronic technicians, lay there, dressed in suits, wearing lead masks that obscured their faces. Alongside them were a notebook, a bottle of water, and two wet towels.

These weren't your typical masks. They were homemade, roughly cut rectangles of lead with holes for eyes, resembling something between an ancient Egyptian death mask and a crude welding visor. These masks bore an uncanny, haunting aura, raising questions about their purpose.

The notebook, written in Portuguese, contained cryptic instructions and phrases. One of the messages read, "16:30 be at the agreed-upon place. 18:30 swallow capsules. After effect, protect metals wait for mask signal." It was a cryptic set of guidelines that seemed to hint at a secretive rendezvous, chemical ingestion, and a signal that was never explained.

The Investigation

As authorities delved into the case, they uncovered more mysteries than solutions. Autopsies revealed no signs of foul play or violence; the cause of death was ruled as asphyxiation. What led two seemingly rational individuals to venture to a remote hilltop, ingest an unknown substance, and don lead masks before their demise remained an enigma.

The Vintem Hill case has given birth to a plethora of theories, ranging from the mundane to the extraordinary. Some believe the two men were involved in a secret cult, following esoteric rituals that required the masks and the ingestion of mysterious capsules. Others speculate that they were testing an experimental drug or attempting to make contact with extraterrestrial beings, explaining the waiting for the "mask signal."

The most plausible theory revolves around the ingestion of a hallucinogenic substance. It's possible that Cruz and Viana were experimenting with a mind-altering drug, a common practice during the 1960s counterculture movement. This could explain the strange messages and the waiting for a signal. However, without further evidence, this remains speculative.

Conspiracy theories have also emerged, suggesting that the men might have been involved in secret government experiments or stumbled upon classified information. Some even propose a link to UFO sightings in the area, positing that they were trying to make contact with extraterrestrial beings.

Despite decades of speculation and investigations, the Lead Masks of Vintem Hill remain an unsolved riddle.

The Dead Walk - The Peculiar Origins of Zombies

The concept of zombies, reanimated corpses devoid of free will, has captivated and terrified people for centuries. While zombies are now iconic figures in popular culture and horror fiction, their origins can be traced back to a complex blend of African, Caribbean, and Haitian folklore, as well as the enduring legacy of slavery, colonialism, and fear of the unknown.

African Roots and Ancestral Spirits

The roots of the zombie myth can be found in the diverse cultures of Africa, where beliefs in the connection between life, death, and the spirit world have been central for millennia. Various African tribes and cultures held beliefs about the dead returning to the world of the living, often as benevolent ancestral spirits. These spirits, known as "ndoki" or "zombi," were thought to provide guidance and protection to their living descendants.

The Transatlantic Slave Trade and Vodou

The African diaspora, resulting from the transatlantic slave trade, brought these rich cultural traditions to the Caribbean, particularly the island of Haiti. It was in Haiti that these beliefs merged with the indigenous Taino culture and the influence of European colonialism to give rise to what we now know as Vodou.

Vodou, a syncretic religion, incorporates elements of African spirituality, Catholicism, and indigenous traditions. Within Vodou, the concept of zombification took on a more sinister connotation. Practitioners, known as "houngans" or "mambos," were believed to possess the power to reanimate the dead, turning them into obedient, soulless labourers called "zombi" as a form of punishment or to serve the interests of the houngan.

The American Imagination
In the 20th century, zombie folklore evolved again as it was introduced to the United States. Early portrayals of zombies were often inspired by Haitian Vodou traditions and depicted them as mindless, enslaved labourers under the control of sinister masters. These themes of oppression and loss of identity resonated with the anxieties of the era, particularly during times of war and economic hardship.

Hollywood's Influence
Hollywood played a pivotal role in shaping the modern zombie archetype. Films like George A. Romero's "Night of the Living Dead" (1968) established the familiar image of the zombie as a flesh-eating, reanimated corpse. Romero's zombies, while inspired by Vodou traditions, became a symbol of societal collapse and the horrors of conformity.

Contemporary Zombie Lore
Today, zombies are a staple of popular culture, appearing in literature, films, video games, and television series. While they have departed from their Vodou origins, the fear of an apocalyptic, mindless horde endures. Modern zombie stories often serve as allegories for societal anxieties, including pandemics, consumerism, and the erosion of individuality.

Fatal Follies - Absurd Deaths in History

Life is a mysterious journey filled with laughter and folly, and sometimes, the curtain falls in the most peculiar and comedic ways. History has a knack for delivering deaths so unusual and absurd that they could be mistaken for the plots of dark comedies.

A Hairy Situation

This story begins in the picturesque town of Braunau am Inn, Austria. The year was 1567, and Hans Steininger had recently been elected as mayor for a historic sixth consecutive term. Beside his extraordinarily long political tenure, Steininger was also admired for the legendary length of his beard! Measuring no less than 48-inches, the facial foliage of Hans was constantly the talk of the town; it had to be rolled up in his pocket at all times, else it would become entwined with the world around him.

Unfortunately, in spite of being both superhumanly popular and hairy, disaster would strike on the 28th of September, 1567. A raging inferno stormed through the idyllic village, and in an effort to save his townsfolk, Hans forgot to tame his beastly beard, which coiled around his ankles as he descended a flight of stairs. The mythically maned mayor was thrown down the stairs, breaking several bones along the way, and tragically passing away.

Still! His memory, and beard, live on in the district museum to this day. For a small fee, visitors to the Branau am Inn Museum can ogle at the murderous beard and pay their respects to its owner-turned-victim.

Objection!

Clement Vallandigham was a well respected politician and lawyer on the American frontier. On the 17th of June 1871, Vallandigham was appointed with the defence of a man accused of murder. The method of the supposed murder; a gunshot to the head. During an emotional appeal to the jury, Clement took it upon himself to demonstrate how the deceased might well have accidentally blown their own head off, and in doing so, accidentally blew *his* own head off.

The unusual, and hopefully accidental, appeal appeared to work, as Vallandigham's client was subsequently acquitted and discharged.

Sleight of Hand

Late 1808, the world must have seemed a dark and uncertain place. Still, in the cold confusion of a pre-industrial, post-war England, a young worker named John Cummings found some respite in watching circus performers act. One such exhibition was a knife swallower, and a good one at that, if Cummings' subsequent actions are anything to go by.

Following the performance, and seemingly failing to understand the illusion at play, John decided to forgo sense and swallow some knives of his own. Impressively, he first swallowed 4 pocket knives, passing three of them with no adverse effects, and evidently feeling quite pleased with himself. The knife swallowing antics rapidly escalated; John next publicly swallowed 14 knives, and after a few days of a sore stomach, passed all of them.

By this time, Cummings was seemingly delighted by the adulation of his act, and finally decided to swallow no less than 20 knives in a single gulp. This time, the blades did not pass. Nor did John. He spent the next 5 years in abdominal agony, before eventually succumbing to internal bleeding.

His autopsy revealed a myriad of trinkets nestled in his gut. Among them were a kitchen knife, a spring, and as many as 40 shards of horn, wood, and metal.

The Show must go on

Jean-Baptiste Poquelin, better known by his stage name, Molière, was a well known and highly respected playwright in 17th century France.

On the 17th of February 1673, during a performance of his own magnum opus, *Le Malade Imaginaire*, Molière, who was playing the role of the titular hypochondriac, was suddenly struck with a major pulmonary haemorrhage, due to complications in the treatment of his tuberculosis. Ingeniously, the Frenchman used the deathly convulsions to his advantage, working them into his performance as the passionate fros of a madman. Molière tragically passed, seated centre stage, as the curtains draw, and a wave of applause rose through the crowd. In a truly bizarre twist, his life very much imitated his art.

Winning the Battle, Losing the War

In the 9th century, few people were more reviled or feared than the terrifying sea-conquerors known as the Vikings. One such warrior was the second Earl of Orkney, Sigurd the Mighty. Known for his battlefield brutality, and heroic exploits, the Norse Earl was deserving of his reputation.

In 892 A.D., after a fierce Norse campaign against the Gallic Scots, Sigurd had secured a major victory against the clans, and taken the head of a revered chieftain, Máel Brigte. In an act of mockery, the Northman strapped his foes head to his horse's saddle. However, in a revenge plot from beyond the grave, as Sigurd rode across the rocky terrain of the highlands, his enemy's teeth bit into his leg. According to some accounts, the wound rapidly grew horrifically gangrenous, and bought Sigurd's reign of terror to an unusual end.

Committed to the Cause

Charondas was a Sicilian politician and lawyer in Ancient Greece. In the early 6th Century B.C. political unrest was so widespread that Charondas proposed a new law; anyone caught carrying weapons into the law-giving Assembly ought be put to death. Initially, the new law was well received.

However, in 612 B.C. Charondas burst into the Assembly-hall begging for help; he'd been violently beset by brigands who sought his wealth. Unbeknownst to the Sicilian, in his panic, he'd unwittingly fetched a knife into the room, strapped around his belt. In a desperate plea not to appear hypocritical, and break a law the he himself had set, Charondas dramatically took his own life before his fellow lawgivers.

A Royal Christmas Pudding

Born into royalty on the 10th of October 1332, Charles II of Navarre was destined to be influential. Unfortunately for him, and even more so for those around him, Charles was birthed into a dynasty at war. He was not a popular man, to say the least. In 1349, he earned the blunt, but direct, moniker "Charles the Bad" after his brutal suppression of a peasant revolt in the Spanish city of Pampeluna. Throughout the course of the Hundred Years' War, the duplicitous King earned an atrocious reputation as a turncoat, bully, coward, and warmonger. He was liked by almost nobody, and so it came as a bizarre matter of jubilation when, in the Yule season of 1386, Charles, aged 54, was taken ill, within the very city he'd crushed years prior. Rumours swirled of the cruel monarch's condition, with almost everyone seeing his diseased state as divine justice, and perhaps they were right. One night, after a great deal of pain, Charles' physicians ordered him to be wrapped in linen, and soaked in distilled spirits, in an effort to warm him. Below the King's ample bed was a small pan, filled with coals. Now you might see where this is going.

Nobody knows exactly how it happened. Some say a chamber maid saw an opportunity and took it, others say it was simply an accident. In any case, the highly flammable, high expensive bedsheets of the maligned ruler took flame, and they lit up the castle within a matter of seconds. The crispy king was set ablaze in an inferno, quite literally, fuelled by his own ill-gotten gains. He officially succumbed to his wounds on the January the 1st 1387, and his divinely driven demise was a matter for immense celebration among his many, many detractors. A warm, cosy way to usher in the new year...

"I do not fear death. I had been dead for billions of years before I was born and had not suffered the slightest inconvenience."
- Mark Twain

Farewell... For now

As we bid adieu to this journey through the dark and twisted corridors of history, I hope that our explorations into the macabre have left you both intrigued and unsettled. The pages of this book have unfurled tales of strange customs, bizarre deaths, and the haunting echoes of yesteryears' horrors.

In the dimly lit alleys of time, we have encountered eccentric characters and gruesome events that challenge our notions of what is ordinary and what is extraordinary. From peculiar punishments to comedic demises, from the ghastly world of body snatchers to the bizarre rituals of ages past, we have ventured into the shadows where history's secrets reside.

As we close the final chapter, remember that history, in all its darkness and eccentricity, is a mirror reflecting the boundless facets of human existence. These stories, while macabre and sometimes unsettling, are a testament to the diversity of human experiences, from the eerie to the inexplicable.

We leave you with these tales as a reminder that the macabre is an integral part of the human tapestry. It serves not only to shock and intrigue but also to teach and caution. It whispers to us from the annals of time, urging us to seek understanding in the most enigmatic and unsettling corners of our shared past.

Though we part ways with these tales, may you carry their haunting echoes with you as you journey onward. For history, even in its darkest moments, is a source of both fascination and illumination. And in the shadows of the past, we find the threads that weave the complex tapestry of human history.

Farewell, dear reader, as you venture forth into the enigmatic realm of history. Let the macabre serve as a reminder that the mysteries of our past are both a source of intrigue and a mirror to our own complex nature.

Acknowledgments

This book would not have been made possible were it not for the unwavering support of my friends and family, who have always encouraged and respected interests and inquiries into the macabre, bizarre, and curious. Were it not for them, I would not possess a true interest in the unusual, nor a sincere ambition to learn from both the mistakes and successes of our shared human past.

This book was written as a tribute to my late grandfather Roger Gillespie (1943 - 2017) who always sought to learn and teach the most valuable of trivial knowledge; to him, all facts were good facts.

Finally, without the incredible artistic contributions of AI, the unique artwork of this book would not have been available. It is absolutely my hope that by collaborating with artificial intelligence, and seeking to understand, rather than fear and abuse, it's power, we may make the world a better, more tolerant, and more educated place.

Bibliography

- Ackerman, Jennifer - The Genius of Birds. *Penguin Press* (2016).

- Borman, Tracey - Witches: A Tale of Sorcery, Scandal & Seduction. *Vintage* (2013).

- Breverton, Terry - Breverton's Phantasmagoria: A Compendium of Monsters, Myths, and Legends. *Quercus* (2011).

- Brooke-Hitching, Edward - Fox Tossing, Octopus Wrestling and Other Forgotten Sports. *Simon and Schuster* (2015).

- Caufield, Catherine - The Man Who Ate Bluebottles: And Other Great British Eccentrics. *Icon Books* (2005).

- Chainey, Dee Dee - A Treasury of British Folklore: Maypoles, Mandrakes and Mistletoe. *National Trust Books* (2018).

- Chainey, Dee Dee & Winsham, Willow - Treasury of Folklore: Woodlands & Forests; Wild Gods, World Trees and Werewolves. *Batsford* (2021).

- Chainey, Dee Dee & Winsham, Willow - Treasury of Folklore: Seas & Rivers: Sirens, Selkies and Ghost Ships. *Batsford* (2021).

- Crofton, Ian - History Without the Boring Bits: A Curious Chronology of the World. *Quercus* (2012).

- Ings, Simon - Stalin and the Scientists: A History of Triumph and Tragedy 1905-1953. *Faber and Faber* (2016).

- Kean, Sam - The Icepick Surgeon: Murder, Fraud, Sabotage, Piracy, and Other Dastardly Deeds Perpetrated in the Name of Science. *Little, Brown and Company* (2021).

- Kerschenbaum, Arik - The Zoologist's Guide to the Galaxy: What Animals on Earth Reveal About Aliens and Ourselves. *Penguin Press* (2020).

- Morris, Thomas - The Mystery of the Exploding Teeth and Other Curiosities from the History of Medicine. *Corgi* (2019).

- Waters, Thomas - Cursed Britain: A History of Witchcraft and Black Magic in Modern Times. *Yale University Press* (2019).

- Whiteley, Aliya - The Secret Life of Fungi: Discoveries from a Hidden World. *Elliott & Thompson* (2022).

Printed in Poland
by Amazon Fulfillment
Poland Sp. z o.o., Wrocław
23 October 2023

dcf20ef0-cdaf-4da5-a8ff-93fec90185a5R01